CW00646019

# TVR
# MUSCLE *and* CURVES

*AN AUTHORISED HISTORY of TVR 1975-1994*

First published 1994


ISBN 1 899369 00 7

Published by **Mitchell-Filby Ltd.,**
**1 Howard Road, Reigate, Surrey RH2 7JE.**
**Tel: 0737 247922**

Typeset by Crocodile
Page design by Jane Shales
Repro by Digiscan
Printed by Creative Press (Reading) Ltd.

# Contents

# Introduction

I did ask Peter Wheeler if he'd like to write the introduction to this book, but he suggested I bog off and write it myself as it was my book anyway. However, he did say he quite liked it, so it looks as that's all we're going to get as far as an endorsement goes. However, on the up side, it's more than Kitty Kelley ever gets, isn't it?The idea was to write a sister volume to Peter Filby's earlier book about TVR, entitled *Success Against the Odds*. This was written in 1975, and told the story of the company from its inception in 1947 through to when the book was published.

Peter's book is rather sought after these days, with copies rumoured to be changing hands at £80 or £90, so it is our intention to publish it again in a new edition. However, for the moment, and for those who are too impecunious to stretch to buying both books, I have squeezed most of the salient facts from Peter's book into the first chapter of this one.

While there is a narrative thread running through this book, it is somewhat more, shall we say, scattered than *Success Against the Odds*. This is partly because TVR as a business has been very stable for the last twenty years, first under Martin Lilley and then under Peter Wheeler, which means the story is less about the linear history of the company and more about different aspects of it. Also, I'm afraid I'm rather scattered by nature, although I have made a valiant attempt generally to keep to the point.

I hope it's as interesting to read as it was to write.

# Acknowledgements

I have had considerable help and support from all at TVR, and in particular from Ben Samuelson, who provided enthusiasm, food, Madeira and slightly squalid but very welcome accommodation on several trips to Blackpool. At the factory, Brian Horner, Andy Dearden and James Pillar in particular gave me all the time and help I needed, and even had the grace to laugh at my jokes.Peter Wheeler and Mike Penney took the time to talk to me at length, the people on the shop floor patiently clambered over my tripod when I got in their way, and Ned endorsed my efforts with an enthusiastic lick.

Roger Cook of the TVR club also took the time to tell me about the history and the aims of the Owners' Club, and the advantages of belonging to it: all TVR owners are welcome, and the club's telephone number is 0242 222878.

TVR

Chapter 1

# Success Against the Odds

The TVR story began in Blackpool shortly after the Second World War, when a young and ambitious engineer called Trevor Wilkinson decided to go off on his own and launch a company to build and sell his own cars. The name of the company was arrived at by simply removing the vowels from Trevor's forename. The letters TVR could also be made into a nice looking badge, so the name stayed – eventually to become world famous as one of Britain's greatest sports car marques.

As described by author Peter Filby in the companion volume to this book, *Success Against The Odds*, Trevor Wilkinson's first special hit the road in 1947 in Beverley Grove, South Shore, Blackpool. The sun shone on a young and enthusiastic Trevor, as he hacked the bodywork off an old Alvis Firebird and replaced it with a two-seater aluminium sports body of his own design.

This exercise made the Alvis perform a lot better, but it was still in the end just a rebodied Alvis, and Trevor was increasingly taken with the idea of building his own car entirely from scratch. However, this is an expensive exercise, and Trevcar Motors had to buckle down to repairs and general engineering to keep some food on the table as well as preparing for things to come. The engineering side of the business was to support the sports car side for several years to come.

***Above: TVR Number One. Stubby and purposeful with quite a complex frame and rock hard suspension, this is where it all started. Below left: The TVR Sports Saloon of 1954, with a long, delicate and quite pretty RGS Atalanta body. This may have started the TVR tradition of tiny doors.***

Even in the early days, the sort of projects that came up reflected the streak of eccentricity that has run through TVR from the beginning. A device for making Easter eggs was one of the items that helped fund the first chassis, and the next year saw a departure into the manufacture of mouth organs and the arrival of Jack Pickard.

By 1949, there was enough money to start construction of the chassis for the first genuine TVR. The first chassis was a simple steel multi-tube affair, with trailing arms at the front and semi-elliptic springs supporting a live axle at the back. The 10 HP engine from a Ford van

***Above: A very early Coupe. Not the most elegant of shapes, but it does have a certain stubby charm. Below: The Grantura Mk3, with an attempt at a styling line above the wheels. Access via the tiny doors is still restricted to thin, fit people.***

provided the engine, and the axle was courtesy of a Morris 8. The aluminium bodywork was constructed by Les Dale, and the not quite finished car was tested with more enthusiasm than caution. Unfortunately the brakes weren't one of the finished parts of the car, so it crashed, setting a trend for the future. Fortunately, it also set a second trend for the future; while TVRs do have a tendency to crash quite a lot, they also have a tendency to stay very much in one piece when crashed, and to protect their owners from the consequences.

The first TVR was sold in 1949, and the resultant £325 was immediately put to work to develop the second TVR, which featured wishbone front suspension. By 1951, the Austin A40 provided the whole mechanicals of the cars, and they began to do rather well in motor sport, particularly in hill climbs.

1953 saw a change of style: the mechanicals were still from the A40, but the chassis had been simplified and was now fitted with a proprietary body made from the revolutionary new Glass Reinforced Plastic. The first such body fitted to a TVR was the RGS Atalanta, and very pretty it was too. There was also

*Above: TVRs in competition. A brace of Mk.3 Granturas are lined up for the off at Le Mans. Unfortunately they boiled up every time they got to the end of the Mulsanne straight, and the end result was a humiliating retirement after three laps. Left: The Mk 2A Grantura featured such luxuries as opening quarterlights, and was powered by either Ford or MG engines.*

***Top: This is a more representative picture of TVRs in competition – the 1966 Tholt-y-Will hillclimb, and Gerry Marshall charges round a hairpin, hanging the tail out in his usual extrovert style. Above: A Mk.3 1800S, with the traditional tiny doors, and non-standard tail lights. In 1967 they should probably have been Mk.1 Cortina Ban-the-Bomb items.***

the option of a body from the Rochdale company, but the styling of the Rochdale bodies was novel rather than attractive.

At this point, the TVR Sports Saloon was available in kit form for £650, and offered the enthusiast a 0-60 mph time of 13 seconds and a top speed of 90 mph: a pretty respectable performance for the time. The mechanical options also began to open up. The faithful Austin A40 could still be plundered, but as alternatives you could now fit the 10 horsepower Ford engine, the 1500 MG unit, or a 2½-litre Lea-Francis.

As the speeds and performance went up, the handling requirements also rose, and the first recognisable TVR chassis became available in 1955. The semi-spaceframe chassis had the still current massive tubular backbone with small seats set low on either side of it. Suspension was courtesy of VW, with trailing arms and torsion bars all round. The suspension was certainly independent: unfortunately it also tended to display a certain independence from the driver's intentions when the car came to a corner.

Times began to change. Making cars as a cottage industry has its place, but the rising demand for Trevor's product meant he had to get serious about premises and plant in order to increase production. Bernard Williams came in with some development money and took a directorship; Fred Thomas also provided a considerable amount of development capital. Ray Saidel started America's on-off love affair with the TVR, importing some Coventry Climax powered chassis to New Hampshire for competition.

1956 saw the first TVR-made GRP body, a stubby open affair with a Rochdale front at either end. This was later fitted with a Ford Consul windscreen and a coupé roof, in which form it went down well in New York. The roof soon evolved into a fastback, and the first recognisable TVR shape was defined.

The TVR Mk1 was in production from 1958, and the engine options were Coventry Climax, the sidevalve Ford 100E or OHV 105E, or the MGA 1500. There were now ten staff, and two cars a month were being made. Ray Saidel was selling them in the States as the Jomar Mk2 for $3995, and there was a lot more demand than supply.

The car gobbled up development money, and a new company, Layton Sports Cars, was formed. The wealthy and enthusiastic Bunty Scott-Moncrieff joined a total of seven directors. Selling the cars was easy, but organising production was a problem that would lead to one disaster after another. By 1959, the staff numbers had risen to 18 and production had actually decreased to one car a month. Ray Saidel, having run out of patience, said the hell with it, and left them to it.

Fred Thomas was removed as MD, and it was something of a shock to Trevor Wilkinson to realise that he was no longer in charge of his destiny. He was still insisting that the car needed more development, while all the rest of the directors were trying in vain to get production under way. Between the middle of 1958 and the end of 1959, only 54 cars were made.

By 1960, production was finally showing signs of real progress, and the 277 orders in January looked promising. Australia, Italy and Malaya were all clamouring for cars, and Colin Escott's first-in-class placing heralded the beginnings of racing success. Staff numbers rose to 43, and the new 1340cc Ford Classic engine was available to fit the restyled Grantura Mk2. Trevor was innovating cheerfully away developing the possibilities of the car – could the Daimler V8 be persuaded to cram itself into the engine bay? No, as it turned out. (A real shame, that.)

With the costs of the growing company still rising exponentially, Arnold Burton of Burton Tailoring was invited with several others to join the Board and contribute to the spending of money, and John Turner was employed to handle the development work. Wasn't that Trevor's department? Well yes, but Trevor had by now been comprehensively elbowed aside, and was no longer really relevant. Production was now 25 cars a month, but unfortunately orders had now dropped to 15 cars a month.

1962 found the Grantura Mk2A on offer, with minor styling changes and some improvement in the sales figures. Quality control was still iffy, and TVR's reputation in the UK was beginning to pose a problem. The Grantura Mk 3 did show some real improvement, with Triumph Herald-based independent wishbone suspension with disc brakes at the front, an independent TVR rear end, and a stiffer chassis with a bigger central tunnel. 500 cars had been made in total, and Trevor had given up. Money was still haemorrhaging in large amounts: an ambitious works team of three cars was sent to Sebring. Unfortunately, one broke an axle, the second broke an engine, and the third crashed.

The ebullient and forceful Brian Hopton was now pushing the company onward and upward, with many grand schemes. Massive orders were supposed to be on the way from the States, and production was geared up to meet the supposed demand. In 1962, a TVR finished the Tulip Rally, but the works team of three cars sent to compete at Le Mans all overheated and retired in an embarrassingly short time. The UK market had been ignored, and the huge US orders failed to materialise. With 90 staff employed, and debts of £77,000, the TVR company went spectacularly bust.

Grantura Engineering Ltd, however, was not bankrupt, and five of the original TVR directors headed by Bernard Williams bought the moulds and a few bits and pieces from the receiver. Sometimes expediency led to the borrowing of a few more bits from the company stores, reputedly resulting in a most ungentlemanly outburst from a chap employed by the receivers to provide an inventory of the remaining assets. One car a week emerged from Grantura, and an American called Dick Monnich helped by ordering a few and paying for them in advance.

Things began to look up, and a few more of the original directors reappeared. The MGB engine was a new option, giving 110 mph performance. Another American dealer, Jack Griffith, began to show an interest, and in fact concocted the first truly evil TVR. Griffith's garage was doing some work on a Cobra owned by the racing driver Mark Donohoe, and the Ford 289CI V8 from the Cobra found its way into Griffith's TVR. It only just fitted, but it did go in. The result was an absolutely wicked car, considerably faster than the Cobra, which was itself no slouch. The car would do sixty in five seconds, and topped out at 160 miles an hour. The Salisbury diff usually found in

***A rare shot of the TVR Trident convertible. The wedge front shows the way ahead. The dog may also be a portent for the future. Or possibly not.***

***Above: The Tulip Rally, 1962, and a works Mk 2A Grantura with an MG engine is piloted by Anne Hall and Val Domleo to a respectable result. Below: The prototype Tina, designed to use rear engined Hillman Imp running gear. Although temperamental, the all-alloy 875cc Imp engine would have made the Tina fast and economical as well as pretty.***

Jaguars was used in the back, and the Griffith sat purposefully on fat wire wheels.

A chap called Martin Lilley had a go in one of these Griffiths, which as it turned out was a fateful meeting: both Martin and TVR were to change course completely as a result of his first experience of the ill-tempered but charismatic car.

1963 turned into 1964, with Arnold Burton of Burton Menswear as chairman: the factory was gearing up to make 10 empty Griffiths a week, to be shipped to the States to meet their engines. There was still a trickle of MG-powered cars for the UK market, but not many were built. The memorable circular Ban-the-Bomb Cortina tail lights fitted to the TVRs of that period were not the fruit of a considered styling decision, but the result of a panic to get a car finished the night before a show. Bernard Williams had unwisely left his shiny new Cortina parked outside the factory, and it got robbed.

The extremely military Major Timothy Knott arrived, replete with serious moustache and an attitude. His brief was to get things organised, but the military approach was less than completely successful, and the workforce tended to become alienated rather than motivated. Bernard Williams slid off sideways and formed Grantura Plastics, which sold bodies back to the main TVR company. Quality control was still a big problem with the Griffith, and the car was still not fully developed.

Money had been sunk into a new car, the Trident. This had been designed by Trevor Fiore, who had capitalised on his considerable talent by changing his name from Frost to something more Italian and therefore more convincing. The Fissore design studio was also involved, and the resulting Trident design was intended to use Ford's 289CI V8 when the car was sold in the States.

However, TVR's luck began to turn bad. Jack Griffith wanted the car to be called the Griffith, and went into a big sulk when Arnold refused. A major American dock strike paralysed cashflow, and the UK sales were still minimal. Arnold had no choice; he had to wind the company up to stop the massive haemorrhage of money.

Ironically enough, there was now an increasing level of success in racing, with Martin Lilley, Gerry Marshall and Tommy Entwhistle getting some promising results.

Trevor Fiore, now one of the creditors of the failed company, sold the Trident design to Bill Last, a Coventry TVR dealer. the car went into limited production, using the Austin Healey 3000 as a mechanical basis. On the same small scale, Bernard Williams collected a few bits from the factory and kept making the odd 1800, keeping the wolf from the door by making bodies for the Trident, amongst other things.

Shortly before the company's crash, Martin Lilley and his father Arthur had bought both a Griffith and £1000 worth of shares in TVR. Rather than lose the money, they stumped up another £20,000 and bought what was left of TVR. This consisted of the factory, some machinery, a few staff and an empty order book. However, Martin got stuck in and rooted out an order from Gerry Sagerman in the US, and another order of ten cars for Spain. He went to fetch the Trident prototype from Italy, to be met with some confusion over where it was and what had happened to it. The confusion was shortly explained when Bill Last's Trident appeared at the Racing Car Show in January of 1966.

The Mk4 1800S appeared in July 1966, and featured a revised engine position, a wooden dash, assorted improvements and brakes from a Triumph TR4. These, like much of the other mechanical componentry, had to be bought with cash upfront, as suppliers were becoming a little wary.

However, Martin fought on. Gerry Marshall raced Martin's Griffith through 1966, and did well. The rear hubs kept falling off, but otherwise the car was reliable and very fast indeed. The brakes weren't really

***Martin Lilley with his father Arthur. Against all the odds, they managed to give TVR its first taste of stable management, and got the company in good shape for the future.***

***The Zante. From this angle, it rather looks as though it has been jacked up from behind before it was dry, but the swoopy wedge front was another hint of things to come. The one existing Zante is currently under restoration.***

up to the demands of racing, so Gerry developed a habit of turning the car sideways before a corner to slow it down; he can still be seen doing the same today with the Tuscans.

Tested on the M1, the Griffith got to nearly 170mph before it started to take off. It was crashed several times, but it takes more than a few crashes to finish off a TVR. In the Isle of Man hillclimb, the Griffith came fifth overall against a field of four wheel drive BRMs. It was a question of having enough nerve to keep your foot down and enough spare rear hubs to last the day.

With the confusion over the Trident fading into the past, Trevor Fiore worked with Martin Lilley to design the TVR Tina. This was to run on the mechanicals and floorpan of the Hillman Imp, and could have shown some promise. However, internal politics on the manufacturer's part precluded any real progress, and the idea was dropped.

TVR were now making a loss on each car at a sale price of £995, but things were steadying, and the TVR 1800S as a car was becoming more established. Through 1966 and 1967, the factory settled down to the slow business of recovery.

Martin Lilley's original Griffith crashed again, and was rebuilt and sold. It crashed again and was rebuilt again. During that period, the first Tuscan evolved, possibly as a result of the Griffith spending so much time in pieces back at the factory. The new Tuscan featured the same mechanical basis as the Griffith, but was more of a wood and leather touring car than an out and out monster. Six were made for the UK, and 28 went to America. Just to keep tradition alive, Gerry Marshall crashed his 1800S demonstrator at a wedding, with the total loss of a Moss Bros top hat.

1967 came and went. Doors got bigger, and the Tuscan wheelbase was extended. 27 more were made. The Targa was prototyped and abandoned. The Gem, with a pretty rear end but a rather peculiar front, was likewise prototyped and abandoned. Sales were still poor, but the character of the cars still kept the faith; one was returned because it 'handled funny'. On test, it confirmed this by spinning off the road and finishing up in a field, muddy but undamaged. When it was retrieved, it handled fine: fair enough, job done.

The Vixen S1 now appeared, visibly the next generation of the same car. It was powered by a 1600GT Ford crossflow engine that gave it 88 BHP and 110 mph. Enduring the year of 1967 had cost £47,000 but the future now looked reasonably promising. Production concentrated on the Vixens through 1968, and the company's financial fortunes began to turn the corner. The Tuscans got a wider body, an updated shape, and a Boss Mustang engine: however, they still made a loss, so they also got the elbow. The increasingly businesslike Lilley was learning fast. Moulding and all GRP work was brought in-house to save money, and as orders rose, overnight working became quite common.

75 detail improvements heralded the launch of the Vixen S2, which was then available for £1250 in kit form and £1583 as a turnkey car. The fifty staff of TVR in that year produced a total of 200 cars.

The following year found the 3-litre Ford V6 fitted to the Tuscan V6, providing a 0-60 time of eight seconds and a top speed of 125 mph: 1969 also found TVR moving into profit, and gearing up to move to bigger premises.

The new Bristol Avenue factory was big enough to allow a good number of cars to be produced, and in fact even twenty years later, it's still big enough for most of TVR's activities to take place there. With a bit of breathing space available to work in, a new chassis was developed for the Vixen. The new 'M' chassis remained very similar to the old one, but it was stronger and it finally rid the car of the occasionally vicious steering kickback from which it had suffered.

While the new chassis was settling into production with the old bodies still being fitted to it, the new 'M' series body was approaching the moulding stage. The new body was longer and smoother, with more room at the tail and the spare wheel mounted in the nose, forward of the engine, rather than taking up all the space in the boot area. The 1300cc engine size option became available, but was received by the public with the same tidal wave of indifference that was to engulf the Pinto-powered Tasmin a few years later. People seem to want their

*Left: The Tuscan V8, a total maniac of a car, with a 4.7 litre Ford engine and a top speed of nearly 170mph. Visually the only difference from a Vixen was chromed window surrounds and a habit of vanishing in clouds of tyre smoke. Above: Much more sensible, but still respectably quick – a 3000M, with the spare mounted in the long nose.*

TVRs with proper engines in, the bigger the better.

The SM or Zante was another prototype, with a tidy front and quite a wild back end. The whole tail swept up and finished in a glass panelled tailgate. However, the Lotus Elite managed the same idea with rather more grace, and the SM never made it into production.

The 2500cc Vixen, powered by the six-cylinder Triumph engine fitted to the TR6, offered respectable performance and a lovely engine note, and did good business for Gerry Sagerman, now TVR's man in the States. TVR's staff now numbered 70, and the company was in good shape. During 1972, the 1300 option was quietly dropped, and October saw the introduction of the 3000M, featuring the three-litre V6 Ford engine used for the Capris and Granadas of the time.

1973 saw the limited edition 3000ML model – a little celebration for Martin Lilley – combining walnut and Wilton with a decent sized engine, and pointing the way forwards. In the same year, TVR achieved the distinction of building the first car ever to be steerable after being smashed face first into a concrete block in a Government safety test. Concrete block? 30mph? No bother.

Solid growth continued through 1974, with output up to between 7 and 9 cars a week. The UK market went through a deep recession, but 85% of TVR's production was going for export anyway. Even with a big strike at BL interfering seriously with the production of the 2500M, TVR managed to build 420 cars in that year.

As we now know, the TVR marque was to enjoy a continuous rise to prominence and success, facing and dealing with many problems along the way. The early Seventies were shaping up to be an unprecendented run of success and rocketing sales figures. Given the company's earlier history, was this too good to be true?

You would be correct in being suspicious that all was going rather too well, in view of the early history of the company. Right enough, in early 1975, fate obliged with a factory fire that stopped production dead. It also put Martin Lilley in hospital with pneumonia, as smoke inhalation joined forces with with the flu with which he had been in bed when the fire brigade called.

Chapter 2

# Towards the Taimars

The fire caused serious problems, but the company fought back and had things under reasonable control relatively quickly. TVR's years of financial shambles and a different number of directors every month had long gone. By 1975, Martin Lilley had been running TVR for ten years as a private company. In fact, only Morgan had a more stable ownership history.

Martin still road tested every car himself, and a large proportion of each car was still made under one roof. Mike Bigland, the technical director, had made a jig on which one could turn out two chassis every day. The chassis was substantial, with the main members in 14 gauge round tube steel and the supporting members in 16 gauge. The front wishbones were made in-house from 12 gauge cold drawn seamless tubing. The internal surface of the chassis tubing was soaked in oil, and then the tubing was capped; then as now, TVRs were built to last.

The smallest engine option on 'M' series cars, reintroduced in response to the fuel crisis of the early Seventies, was the 1600 OHV four cylinder Ford engine as fitted to the Capri. In the relatively light TVR, this still gave a pretty respectable performance. I've been on a speed trial in a 1600 Vixen, and it was keeping up with some pretty exotic competition. Its main limitation was the strength of the driver's wrists, as the steering kickback under extreme thrashing was a little like hanging on to the ankles of a rabid buffalo. The next engine size up was the Triumph 2500cc six, fitted with twin Strombergs and putting out around 106 BHP, depending on the amount of smog gear fitted. The 2500M, featuring the smogged TR6 engine, was exported in significant numbers to

***The Vixens all shared the same bodyshell, decor and trim. With a relatively small bore exhaust system visible underneath, this one is probably the 1600cc Ford powered model.***

*Above: The 2500cc Triumph engine, drive train and TR6 diff, all mounted in a Vixen rolling chassis. Steering and brakes are also mostly Triumph. Below: A 2500 Vixen, distinguishable by the 2500 badges on its sills. This one sports a sunbathing naturist on the bonnet: this is probably because the car is a lot warmer than the grim-looking Blackpool beach.*

the States. In October of 1975, 250 of them were ordered for America.

The straight six engine had already been federalised by Triumph for use in their own US export cars. However, although by no means a bad engine, the Triumph six had political problems. Due to Leyland's tendency to down tools with distressing frequency, the availability of the engine was always rather dodgy, and Martin Lilley was wary of the problems this could cause. Industrial relations at TVR, then as now, featured the occasional row, but no strikes.

Part of Martin's response to the Leyland problem was to stockpile large numbers of the engines – three months' worth, in fact. However, this was expensive and it only offered limited protection from a big strike. The second alternative was to federalise the Ford V6 used in the 3000M. Ford had never intended the engine for the US, so it wasn't available in smogged form. The matter became more urgent when Triumph axed the TR6 and stopped making sports cars. The cosmetically

challenged TR7 featured a new and dull four-cylinder engine, suitable for shopping cars rather than TVRs.

The Ford 'Essex' 3-litre used in the 3000M was federalised by Olsen in California, and very successfully; the performance figures for the detoxed engine were very similar to the UK cars. If the emissions could get through the Californian tests, it would be squeaky clean as far as the rest of the USA was concerned. The car sold well in this form, and remained available with that engine until 1979.

To a great extent, the 3000M carried on in a similar form during its life. The differential changed from the original TR6 with Triumph 2000 driveshafts to the Salisbury 4HU axle, as fitted to the Jaguars of

*Above: The rear end of the Vixen chassis. In the foreground is one of the dodgy aluminium suspension uprights so beloved of Gerry Marshall. Left: Lined up outside the factory in about 1973, these TVRs represent the transitional stage between the Vixen and the M series cars. In the foreground is a 2500M, still powered by the Triumph six but with the later, longer bonnet. Below: An early V6 3000M, still featuring Mk.II Cortina door handles. The engine bay air outlet duct was originally intended to grace the rear pillars on the very same Cortina.*

the time. The methodology of building the cars had settled down, and quality control was improving. The bodies were cured three times in an oven at 140 degrees, which got most of the bubbles out of the gelcoat. A neat touch from the production point of view was that the bodywork had been designed to be ambidextrous – RHD and LHD bodies came out of the mould exactly the same, and you just cut the appropriate holes according to the nationality of whoever had ordered the car.

With 45 employees producing about six cars as week, the company was increasingly efficient; the UK market was quietly rising, and exports went as far

***Above: With the bulk of a Ford V6 crammed into the 3000M engine bay, there's not much room left over. Right: Stewart Halstead on the track. Even with the limitations of the small iron V6, the M series TVRs could put up a respectable performance in competition. Below: 3000M rolling chassis, with the Ford V6 nestling neatly in the engine bay. The diff is now a much bigger and meatier affair, and the new M series chassis has also visibly evolved.***

afield as Panama and Japan.

A reviewer of a 1600M objected to the gear lever being too far back, necessitated by the mid-front placing of the engine, and noted the problem of getting luggage aboard. Otherwise he was generally very impressed by the comfort and trim of the car, and thought that the chassis was far too good for the engine. The brakes were apparently outstanding when fitted to a TVR, although the same set-up in the TR6 was nothing special.

Competition in terms of sales came from the Ford Capri, Datsun 240Z, Reliant Scimitar, Lotus Elite and so on. Competition on the track came from Morgan, Jaguar E-Types and the Lotus Europa. In the hands of Stewart Halstead, Colin Blower and Rod Gretton, TVR were more than holding their own. Many outright wins were recorded in the BRSCC and BRDC Prodsports series.

The press, the owners and all and sundry had been complaining about the lack of a hatchback for years, and finally Martin gave in and hinged the big rear window. This sea change was marked by a new name for the car – the Taimar.

Apart from the hatch, the Taimar was very little altered from the 3000M. The suspension setting were altered slightly, and there was another of the periodic

***Above: The Taimar's rear hatch was a useful size and made the car a much more practical proposition. The owner seems to have forgotten her frock. Below: Martin Lilley looking pleased with himself. As well he might: so would most of us if we had two Ferraris and a TVR Convertible on the drive.***

*Right: The long nose of the M series cars allowed a full size spare to be carried under the bonnet, as well as Ford's injection gear. Below: Making it into a Convertible seems such an obviously sensible thing to do to a TVR: it's extraordinary that it took them so long to get around to it.*

rearrangements of the dash and heater system, and some improvements in the ventilation. At £6223, the TVR was £2000 more than the three-litre Capri, and £500 more than the Datsun 240Z. However, the handling was in a different league from the sporty saloons, and the performance from the V6 was respectable, with 0-60 times of 8.2 seconds, a top speed of 127 mph, and an overall mpg of about 22.

The strong mid-range performance made the car particularly good for high speed cross-country driving, although at low speeds and over rough surfaces it was still less than entirely poised. The chassis and engine were to remain as they were for some time, as variations on the theme were explored.

Having accepted the idea of cutting a hole in the back for a hatch, the next obvious move was to cut the roof off. If this is done to a thin steel monocoque, the result handles something like a beached whale, but with the rigid tubular backbone under the TVR, it made a minimal difference to the dynamics of the car whether it had a roof or not.

However, the job was more involved than just cutting the top off. The chassis and bonnet remained the same, as did the floorpan and interior arrangements, but from the screen back, everything else changed. The doors were completely different, and featured sliding sidescreens in frames that came completely off, leaving a sculpted cutaway to rest your elbow on. The soft top folded back into a space behind the seats, and for the first time a TVR had a boot.

The new screen sat atop a completely redesigned scuttle, which had always been rather high on TVRs. Unfortunately, the central tunnel remained as high as ever, which meant that the instruments could no longer be positioned where they could be read properly.

Colin Blower raced a convertible with considerable success. To be more accurate, he raced more than one, as his first one got comprehensively trashed in a 110 mph crash. "It just rolled and rolled..." Colin untangled himself from what remained and walked away with two cracked ribs; a considerable testament to the inherent strength of the TVR design. In Colin's next convertible he won 22 out of 24 races entered. This was in Prodsports, where the cars are kept pretty well standard apart from safety gear.

Some competition was offered by Morgans, which are very low, very fast and have no visible suspension at all. With a little more suspension and a shorter wheelbase, the TVR had the edge. It was easier to get it into a sideways slide, but the slide could be controlled. This was how Gerry Marshall had coped with racing on standard road brakes, after all; if it wouldn't slow down in a straight line, just turn it sideways.

It was of course an old TVR tradition to make the occasional maniac car, and it had been some years since the 289CI Ford V8 had been shoehorned into a Vixen to create the original Griffith. The idea of turbocharging the V6 had been at the back of various minds for some time, and in 1975 the first prototype was built. Following another hallowed TVR tradition, it

***Below: The main visual difference between the early Convertibles and the later S convertibles was the metal windscreen frame and the detachable side windows.***

was also crashed.

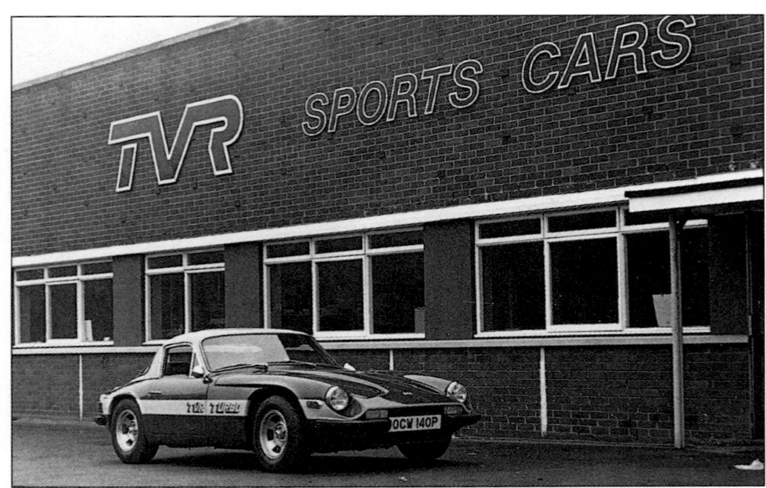


***Top: Early Convertible interior. The high transmission tunnel and low scuttle height meant that the instruments had to be put wherever there was room for them, whether you could see them or not. Above: An early Turbo outside the Blackpool factory. The V6 definitely got a move on when encouraged by the fitting of a turbocharger.***

The turbocharger for the V6 had been replaced by Broadspeed, and the power increase over the standard engine was massive – something like 70%. 230 BHP at 5500 rpm was claimed, and the torque figures went up from 172 to 273 ft/lbs. This was in a car weighing in at some 25 hundredweight. There was deep joy among TVR employees and enthusiasts when a TVR Turbo proved to be half as fast again as a Porsche Turbo.

A fair bit of work had gone into the project; it was far from a simple bolt-on job. The Salisbury axle was used exclusively on the Turbo cars, as it would generally take whatever was handed out to it. The gearbox from the Granada/Capri 3-litre cars was used, as was the Essex V6. This had been improved over the years, and was a lot stronger in its later forms.

The compression was lowered to 8:1, and the engine was blueprinted and balanced. Turbo pressure was 9 psi. The manifolds swept forward rather than back, and the relatively empty space in front of the engine was used for the turbo unit. The pipework then went under the engine and into the airflow for some cooling. The impeller was kept spinning by a recirculating valve, so that the lag between putting your foot down and hitting the back of your seat was kept to a minimum.

Although the emissions from the turbocharged Essex engine were surprisingly clean, there was never an attempt to market the car in the USA. TVR only ever built 63 Turbos, but the splash they made in the consciousness of the motoring public was out of all proportion to their numbers. The magazines lined up to play with them, and usually compared then with Porsches and Ferraris. Favourably too, for the most part; after all, they were always cheaper, and nearly always faster.

Even Stirling Moss, who has seen and done most things, was notably impressed with the Turbo. "An endless, effortless surge of acceleration," he said, in a review which also noted that below the 2700 rpm turbo power band, the car behaved just like an ordinary TVR, and could be used perfectly well as a regular road car.

When the Turbo was put through its paces by an engineering publication, it was reported that the engine could be run continuously at 6250 revs, although it was recommended that upper cylinder lubricant be added to the fuel if the engine were to be exercised at higher revs. Even writing about it in the dullest of engineerese couldn't spoil the fun. 18 mpg was recorded at a continuous 100 mph. It was noted with concern that the fanbelt could not be removed with the turbocharger bracket in place, and it was noted with approval that the ignition cut out when the alternator stopped.

However, they couldn't contain their glee when they got to playing with the brakes. Braking efficiency exceeded 1g, "in the presence of some smell and smoke." Yes, one can imagine. Although the car's handling felt very good on smooth surfaces, it felt much less stable on rough surfaces. However, the underlying stability of the chassis was underlined when a rear tyre punctured during high speed testing; the effect of the puncture was noted as an increase in noise, and more throttle pressure required to maintain 100 mph.

Chapter 3

# The Tasmins

The Tasmin, named after Martin Lilley's inamorata of the time, was the first TVR to bear no resemblance at all to the proportions of the early Grantura, which had given the familiar stubby look to all TVR bodies since the sixties.

The Tasmin was a sharp angular wedge, with a long, deep screen. When it was launched at the Brussels show in January of 1980, it was ahead of nearly everyone else with the sharp-edged design themes of the Eighties. The body design was by Oliver Winterbottom and the chassis by Ian Jones, both of whom were ex-Lotus. However, the light and delicate chassis designs usually found under Lotus bodyshells had little influence, and the beefy TVR tubular backbone tradition continued. The main rails were 14 gauge, and the supporting rails were 12 gauge; wheelbase was 7' 10".

The body was made in two main pieces, which

***The new Tasmin represented a radical departure from the traditional TVR shape, and was way ahead of most manufacturers with the sharp styling lines of the Eighties.***

***Above: Beneath the skin, the new Tasmin chassis had also benefitted from some attention, but was still a light, strong tubular backbone in the true TVR tradition. Below: It wasn't long before a convertible version of the Tasmin became available: it retained the clean, sharp lines of the first Tasmins.***

were then joined together at the waistline. It was mounted on the chassis at twelve points, which kept the interior very well insulated from road and engine noise and vibration. Tubular door bars for impact protection were bonded into the door shells, and the hinges were bonded into the body. Marine quality plywood was used for stiffening and to construct impact beams within the bodywork. A novel and stylish design feature was the glass panel in the tail, which made parking very easy.

The petrol tank had been moved forward, away from the original rather vulnerable position in the tail of the earlier cars, and now featured twin chrome filler caps on two connected tanks. In theory, this meant you could fill the tanks from either side, but in practice the smart move was to open both filler caps to allow the tanks to breathe as they were filled. Average mpg of around 22 combined with a 14 gallon fuel capacity offered a reasonable touring range. The full size spare wheel was now located where the tank had been on earlier cars – right at the tail.

The scuttle was quite high, and the single wiper blade swept a deep and steeply raked screen. The bonnet line was unbroken by headlights, which were electrically powered pop-ups.

There were some nice touches in terms of finish; the bumpers were colour coded to the stripes along the side of the car, and the interior was to quite a high spec. There were no external aerials, as the heating element for the rear hatch was used as a radio aerial.

The interior was heading deliberately upmarket,

with burr walnut dash panels, electric windows and a Sundym screen. There was a stereo fitted as standard, with a full set of instruments consisting of speedo, tacho, oil, fuel, water, volts and clock. The Stewart Warner instruments were of the type that retained their last reading when switched off, which could be initially confusing, as it gave the impression that the entire dashboard electrics had all packed up at once.

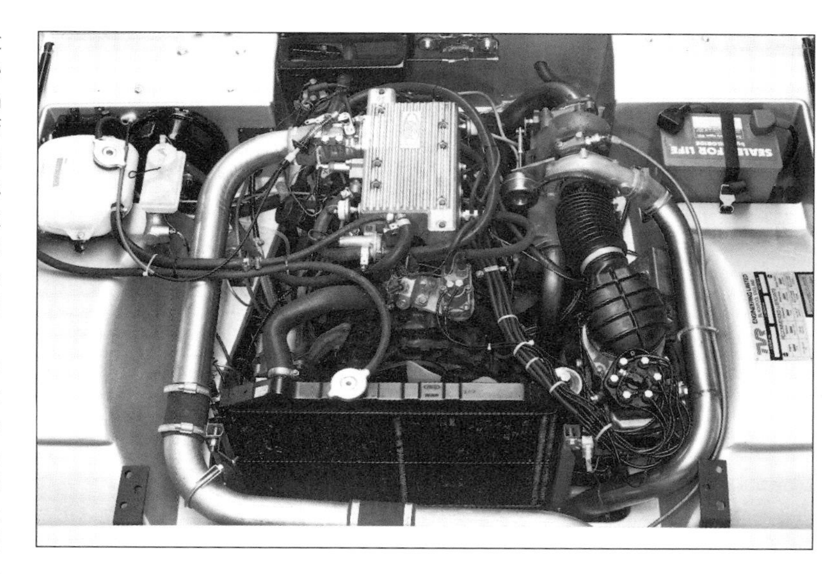

A similar collection of mainstream manufacturers' parts were used, but rearranged to suit TVR. The Tasmin's rear lights and door handles were from the Capri, and the steering column and stalks were British Leyland. The front suspension used Cortina wishbones and track control arms, with bigger Granada uprights and brakes. The leading lower link was changed to a trailing type, and the rack used was from the Cortina. Mounted on posts, it was designed to pull the steering column away from the driver in an impact.

***Above: The fuel injected Ford 280i V6 engine. Custom engine bay pipework is secured by jubilee clips and exhaust clamps, but is none the worse for that. Below: The next model was known as the Series $1\frac{1}{2}$. This one features the $2\frac{1}{2}$ mph bumpers.***

***The Tasmin's interior from day one showed evidence of where the money had gone, with liberal use of walnut and leather.***

At the back, the Salisbury 4HU differential had found a permanent home; it was proved to be up to the job. With a final ratio of 3.07:1, it provided 22.2 mph per 1000 rpm. The 10.9" inboard discs fitted to the Salisbury diff were bigger than the 10.6" discs fitted to the front of the car, but brake line pressure control via a G valve stopped the car swapping ends on braking. The brakes certainly worked – 80 lbs on the pedal would result in a more than 1G stop.

The rear suspension was considerably different from the earlier double wishbones. It consisted of a semi-trailing arm mounted on large rubber bushes, lower lateral links, and TVR's own cast uprights with fixed length driveshafts. The driveshafts were used as the upper links, and were adjustable by shims. Spring travel was long at 7", and the whole suspension system was designed with long distance touring in mind. With the demise of the TR6, Leyland had stopped making Triumph sports cars, and in a helpful move to leave the market wide open for the TVR, they then withdrew the MGB as well. Martin Lilley was after exactly this market with the Tasmin.

Power for the Tasmin remained a Ford V6, but the Essex had now been replaced by the Cologne-built 2.8 litre engine. This was used with Bosch K-Jetronic injection, giving 160 BPH at 5700 rpm. In the relatively light Tasmin, the performance was impressive, as noted by Autosport, who said that the car would "reach and exceed 130 mph in an extraordinarily short time". Gearing was fairly high from the four-speed gearbox, again reflecting the touring aspirations of the car. The gear lever was altered to lean forwards, because of the engine and box being so far back in the chassis.

The Broadspeed derived clutch actuation system in the early cars had the hydraulics inside the bellhousing. This was fine as long as the hydraulics held out, but it meant that replacing a 15p cylinder seal involved taking the engine and gearbox out, which was less than universally popular with the owners; a cable system was introduced in 1980. A more conventional hydraulic system was used later in LHD cars because the cable had to go wandering all over the car to get from the pedal to the slave cylinder, which is usually a recipe for trouble. In my own experience of an Audi Coupe, the only mechanical fault the car displayed in 220,000 miles of problem free thrashing was the annual replacement of a popped clutch cable.

The fuel system for the injected V6 had the pump located under the fuel tank in the airflow to keep it cool. From there, the fuel went through an accumulator and a filter to the metering head. The original tanks were secured with lugs, but these proved unreliable and were replaced with straps. The exhaust, originally a single box, went under the propshaft in early cars. A new stainless steel system placed the main box above the propshaft, but that had the unfortunate effect of cooking the occupants of the car, so it was abandoned in favour of a four-box Langford system, which solved the problems.

The wiring was originally all black, with coloured clips for coding. This sounds like a living nightmare, and it is with no surprise that one notes the reintroduction of coloured wire from January of 1982, along with more fuseboxes reflecting the increasing electrical complexity of the cars.

*An early fixed head Tasmin 280i, showing the sharp lines that the others would soon be following.*

*Above: Resplendent in red, an early 280i convertible. Removing the roof was an excellent idea. Left: The registration mark TVR100 is deeply confusing, as it reappears on various TVR owned cars through the years. Those wheels, on the other hand, came and went quickly.*

*Left: The interior of a Tasmin, opulent with wood and leather. Below: The TVR100 number appears again. This time it's on a 350i convertible shown here at speed, which is after all the natural state for a TVR.*

E666 FHG

*Opposite: With the S Convertible, the more traditional TVR shapes reappeared, offering good value for money. Left: The early interiors for those cars showed what could be done with veneer, rather than what should be done with it. Below: A cutaway view of an S shows the massive tubular backbone chassis common to all TVRs, and still one of the best reasons for buying one.*

*Above: A Haughins prepared supercharged SX350, with the body showing signs of the general future direction of the Tasmin shape. Right: The same car turns a meaty rump to the camera. As Michelotti said, silver is the one colour that brings out the shape of a a car.*

*Above: It was a little ungentlemanly to unleash this monster amongst the sports racers, as it wiped the floor with them until it was banned. Left: A Tuscan racer in fairly lurid livery. Quite apt, really. Below: Colin Blower's successful Tasmin convertible racer, sponsored by Indestructible Socks.*

*The Tasmin shape comes of age. The 280i above is essentially the same car as the 390SE, but the improvement in its looks reflects myriad changes beneath the skin, not least of which is the bored out Rover V8.*

# Chapter 5
# The Prodigal Returns

The big, musclebound TVRs were now heading strongly for £30,000. Peter Wheeler realised that nothing much was on offer for the traditional TVR punter, who wanted a fast, fun sports car but wasn't prepared to exchange his house for it. The answer was to go back a few years and to bring out a convertible that was basically a developed version of the old Taimar theme. The Convertible 'S' retailed at £13,000 – about half the cost of an exotic TVR wedge. Some of the body lines were the same as the later 3000S from the Lilley days, but all the actual panels were new. The chassis was completely different from the old cars. However, brakes were right back in the Sixties with discs at the front and drums at the back, and the windows had to be wound up by hand. The chassis followed the usual TVR backbone design, and was constructed from 2½" rectangular and 1½" round steel tubing. The front suspension comprised TVR wishbones with coilover shocks and a forward running anti-roll bar. The rear suspension consisted of semi-trailing arms, again with coilover shocks, and with sliding variable length driveshafts.

Brakes were all outboard; there were 9" drums at the rear, but the front brakes were 10.3" vented discs with Girling calipers, so the braking performance wasn't a period piece. There was no power steering option, but with 3.5 turns lock to lock, the steering was reasonably light and didn't really need power assistance. Power came from the familiar Granada/Capri injected V6, of 2792cc, fitted with Bosch K-Jetronic fuel injection. With a compression ratio of 9.2:1, the engine produced 150

***A silver paint job brings out the shape of the S. Although the general shape of the car is strongly reminiscent of earlier TVRs, none of the panels remain from the old cars.***

bhp at 5700 rpm, with 162 ft/lb of torque at 4300 revs. The gearbox was standard, and the Sachs rear end with a ratio of 3.58:1 resulted in 24.13 mph per thousand revs.

With the quite slippery shape and light weight of the TVR, this gave a respectable 7 seconds to sixty, and a top speed of 133 mph. The bodywork was mounted on Metalastik bushes, and the one-piece flip front idea was brought over from the earlier cars. Invisible from the outside was some new thinking on body crumple zones, as technology and ideas filtered across from the wedge designs. The spare was now a space-saver stowed in the boot, as the full size road wheel at 7" x 15" with a 205/60 Bridgestone would have taken up all the boot space needed for stowing the targa top. There was a removable panel between the boot space and the cabin, which allowed long objects to be carried. The convertible top wasn't actually a soft top, but a split targa roof, with removable hard panels above both the driving and passenger seats. With the targa panels removed, the rest of the roof folded back into the body.

The S generally went down really well, and predated the Japanese swing to nostalgia by several years. An American review described the S as "a brand new early Sixties sports car" and went on to enthuse at length about the pre-emission control acceleration, and the feeling that he could sense every bump, every change in the surface texture of the road. He was less enthusiastic about the quality control, the bits falling off and the non-functional heater, but recommended that his readers buy the car just for the fun of owning it.

Roger Bell, sorting out the position of the TVR in the marketplace, observed that it "... splits the Lotus

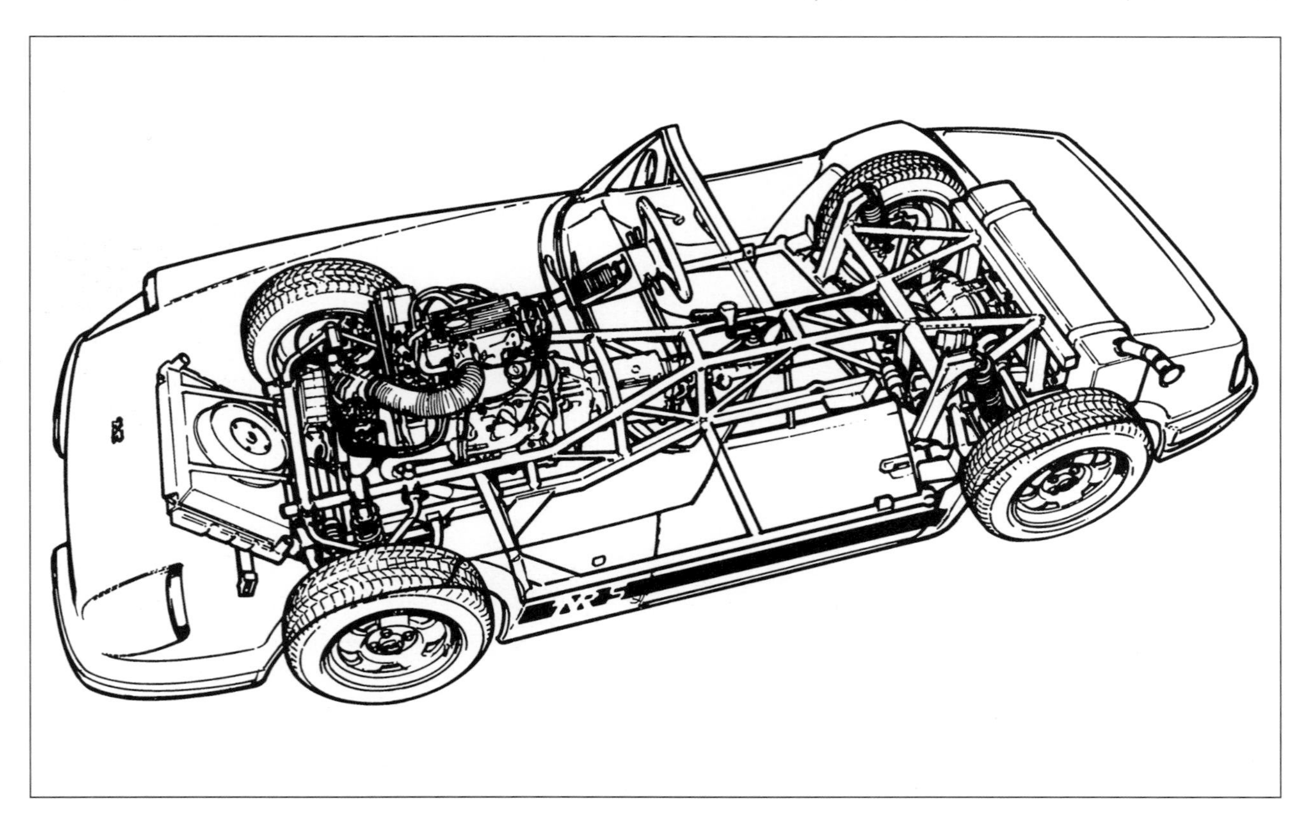

***Below: The chassis of the S follows the American design principle "If it ain't broke, don't fix it." The chassis was an update of the traditional TVR backbone. Above right: Wooden S1 interior from 1981. 'Nuff said.***

Elan and Mazda MX-5 on price, and in certain respect outranks them on ability". He thought the dash was poor, and was undecided about the steering – he liked the sensitivity of it, but was less impressed with its kicking and wriggling. However, this didn't stop him buying an S2 secondhand in 1991.

The six-cylinder S carried on through S2 and S3 forms, with minor improvements in chassis stiffness, footroom and general trim, and the introduction of the 2.9 litre, 168 bhp Cologne V6 engine when it became current. The S3C was fitted with a catalytic convertor, but TVR were careful to fit a big one in order to avoid smothering the performance. In a climate with generally coldish ambient temperatures, there is a view that a catalytic convertor is more effective in keeping the environmental lobby quiet than in keeping the air clean, but whether catalysts are political or environmental engineering, TVR managed to incorporate them into their cars without spoiling the fun.

The fun was certainly not in short supply. Stephen Bayley, reviewing the S3C in *Gentlemen's Quarterly,* was almost beside himself with excitement. A list of the words he used in his description of the car is quite illuminating: 'criminal, brutal, coarse, exhilarating, frightening, attractive, gruff, communicative' and 'bargain'. Mind you, he usually gets to review BMWs, injected shoppers and the like, so it would be a bit of a thrill to get his hands on a proper sports car.

***Above: A rear quarter view shows that the rear part of the hood doesn't fold down into the body, the only problem with an otherwise excellent system. Below: The Ford V6, livened up considerably by the fitting of a fuel injection system. In the crammed hi-tech engine bay of a TVR, the wavy shape of the rocker covers is the clue to the origin of the engine.***

***Above: The S Convertible wasn't*** quite ***as fast as a Lightning, although its performance was respectable by anybody's standards. Below right: Half targa top, showing the folding rear section of the roof. The interior reflects a growing trend to radical, organic shapes, and looks a lot better in leather than it did in wood.***

Peter Tomalin, a died-in-the-wool TVR enthusiast already, said it was the rough and ready 'Here I am, you bastard' style that won the car so many friends. Although the Ford V6 engine had its points, it was basically missing a couple of cylinders and a good few cubic inches, and it suffered from both weight penalties and political penalties in some markets.

There was also Wheeler's typically pragmatic and clear-thinking approach to problem solving. Essentially, if you want to take a bite out of something, you can either use a poodle with rabies, which does the job but doesn't sound too good and won't last all that long, or you can start off with a pit bull terrier in the first place. Of course, if you're Peter Wheeler, you will eventually give in to the temptation to inject the pit bull with rabies as well, and then sit on its back and kick it, but that's another story. The Tuscan story, in fact.

1991 saw the launch of the V8S, fitted with a Rover V8 that ended up quite far removed from the item generally found chugging about in Land Rovers and Range Rovers. The V8 had been developed by what was now TVR Power in Coventry, and was a 3.9 litre version of the Rover engine, with gas-flowed heads, a fast road cam and a compression ratio of 10.5:1. It also featured a fancy set of exhaust manifolds and a reprogrammed chip in the engine management system. The overall results were fairly spectacular. 240 bhp at 5500 rpm, and torque of 270 ft/lb at 4200. The chassis that found its way under the S saw considerable benefits from the experience gained in racing. The exhaust system fitted to the V8S was recognisable as having come from the racetrack, and shows the benefits of lateral thinking. Most exhaust manifolds sweep backwards from the engine, as that's the natural way to think of them. However, TVR manifolds point forwards instead, and then curve down in front of the engine where there's lots of room. This is better than cramming themselves into the space between the engine sides and the chassis rails, where they get in the way, compromise their own gas flow and roast both the starter motor and the driver's legs, a situation with which most Cobra replica owners will be ruefully familiar.

After the original chassis used for the six-cylinder model was superseded by the stiffer and more triangulated chassis developed for the V8, the later chassis became common to both V6 and V8. The

overall track width had been extended by 40mm, and the brakes were changed to discs all round, with bigger, vented discs fitted at the front. The spring and damper rates also benefitted from some revision. A viscous LSD was fitted at the back, and 205/60 ZR rated tyres got the power down to the road. The interior, as is the way with TVR, has been both looked at and seen to at various times in the history of the S, but has usually retained something of the traditional feel in keeping with the shape of the body.

***Above: Luxury wind-up windows: the fake quarterlights look okay with the windows shut. The model has some clothes on, indicating that TVR's advertising strategy was heading upmarket. Below: The interior of an S2 Convertible – a considerable improvement over earlier efforts. Increasingly cosy and practical, and still loaded with wood and leather.***

Acceleration figures were just under 5 seconds to sixty, and 12.4 seconds to 100 mph. *Performance Car* took a V8S to Millbrook for a good thrashing, and achieved 146 mph two up with a full tank. They also achieved some remarkable figures in the perhaps more relevant and certainly more neglected area of 50-70 mph, which is where most overtaking takes place. In those terms, the TVR achieved a figure of 5.9 seconds, making it faster than the Aston Martin Virage, the Ferrari Testarossa, the Lotus Esprit Turbo and the Porsche Carrera 2.

They also tested the car out on the

***Top: The rear end of an S under construction in the Blackpool factory. TVR's own trailing arm and hub locates Ford drivetrain and brake components. Above: The front suspension consists of meaty TVR engineered wishbones with adjustable castor angles, and vented Ford disc brakes.***

***Top: The injected V6 fitted to the chassis. Again, not a lot of spare space, particularly with all the air boxes and injection gear. Above: With the wheels and body on, the general effect is much more convincing. In the background is a Tasmin shell fresh from the paint shop.***

open road, and got an average of nearly twenty miles to the gallon, and that figure included the Millbrook thrashing. Having noted that the rear semi trailing arm suspension had indulged in a little tramping when the clutch was dumped at 5000 for a 5-second run to sixty, they were perhaps expecting a less than 100% handling performance across country. However, the handling proved to be remarkable neutral, with a little understeer as they went into a corner fast, changing to power oversteer on the way out.

Even the high speed dynamics came in for praise, with the ride described as firm but not bumpy, the noise levels as low and the backdraught over the screen as not bad at all. The clever half-targa convertible roof system had come across from the wedge TVRs, and made travelling with the roof up nearly as civilised as if the car were fitted with a hard top.

The only reservations *Performance Car* had about the V8S concerned the messages through the steering wheel on rough roads, which is pretty well traditional on TVRs. However, the concensus of opinion seems to be that it feels a lot worse than it is, and that if you hang on and keep your foot down, the car will do pretty well what it's told, irrespective of the kick and wriggle through the steering wheel. And if the steering at parking speeds is heavy, the feel of it on the road is more than a good tradeoff.

The superlatives from the rest of the Press had progressed beyond the gibbering stage, and were beginning to approach awe. "Totally flat torque curve – the power is just full on all the time ..." "A tidal wave of torque ..." "Everything a British sports car should be ..." "Steroidal" said Roger Bell in *The Independent*. "Rampant, blood and thunder".

He tried to complain about the crude heating, the lack of an anti-lock braking system and the noisy exhausts – "no social conscience about noise abatement" – but his heart wasn't in it.

In 1993 you could still buy both the V6 S4C and the V8S, if you aspired to a serious sports car but couldn't quite stretch as far as a Griffith or a Chimaera. However, the second coming of the Beatle era TVRs was on the wane, and the new and sexy Nineties shapes were attracting all the superlatives and most of the sales.

# Chapter 6

# The Tuscan Challenge

TVR had been involved in motorsport of one sort or another since the very early days. Even the early Granturas with their good power to weight ratio and relatively low centre of gravity put up a respectable performance, despite the VW torsion bar suspension at both ends and the resultant creative input to cornering.

The stiffness, lightness and toughness of the later TVR backbone chassis, combined with hard and technically good suspension, made it generally pretty competitive at club level. In 1980, a 3000M took the Prodsports championship with 22 clear wins.

Colin Blower enjoyed considerable success in TVRs, and did well for his sponsors, Indestructible Socks. When he pranged his first Convertible in a terrifying 100 mph multiple rollover, it is not recorded whether his socks survived the incident, although his underpants probably didn't. However, true to character, the structure of the TVR protected him, and he was able to walk away with only two cracked ribs.

The 1986 racing 420SEAC was disrespectful of the authorities, and ultimately paid the price. The car was faster than anything else on the track, by an absurd percentage. If there was a 420SEAC win a

***The S Convertible racer with a 500bhp Cosworth Turbo RS500 engine and Hewland FGB400 transaxle raced in the Sports Car series, here painted in Tuscan livery to promote the racing series.***

***Above: The David Gerald sponsored 420SEAC racer. Never mind a fox amongst the chickens, this was a grenade lobbed into the henhouse. Below: Colin Blower and the Indestructible Socks Tasmin, pushing his luck. The missing Socks graphic on the replaced front wing suggests he's already pushed it too far at least once.***

race, it would win. By the time the first car that wasn't a SEAC got past the chequered flag, the champagne would already have gone flat.

Needless to say, it was no time at all before the car was banned on homologation grounds, although it was genuinely on sale to the public in pretty well the same form as the racing version. For the next while, a heavily modified S road car fitted with a 500 horsepower Cosworth Turbo engine kept the faith, and did rather well in Modsports. John Kent drove the S, and Steve Cole ran the SEAC.

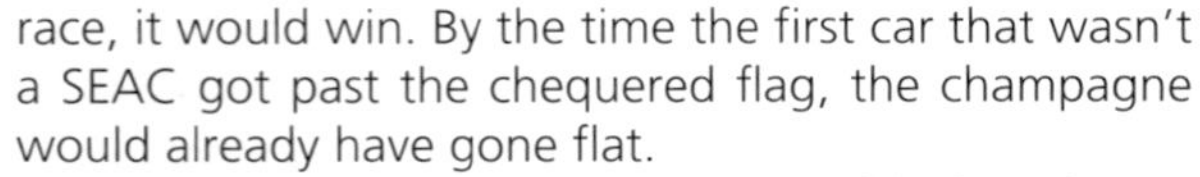

Wheeler, however, had now tasted blood, and he wanted to see his big evil V8 monsters thundering round the track; unfortunately, there wasn't really anything around for them to race against. Fair enough, he thought, if there's nothing around to give TVRs any competition, they'll just have to fight amongst themselves. Now if we take the power and handling parameters of the banned 420SEAC as a starting point, and design a pure racer to do the same sort of thing, but even faster ... and so the Tuscans were born.

The Tuscan challenge was announced in Birmingham at the 1988 Motor Show, and the idea went down a storm. Gerry Marshall: "It'll be a fabulous spectacle, I'm really looking forward to it". The BRSCC were also keen: "This looks like good racing". *Fast Lane* magazine decided to join in rather than just write about it, and entered a car in the series. Having got the sort of response they wanted, all TVR had to do now was to make 35 cars before the season started. With delays on the supply of parts, and no actual extra space in the factory to build the Tuscans, there were a good few all-nighters. Two months of all-nighters, to be precise. Still, as Wheeler says, you only need six hours of sleep a night.

By the time the day of the first race dawned, on May 7, 1989 at Donington Park, there was a respectable grid of Tuscans. One was notably missing, the result of enthusiasm over experience; the car had spun off at a very high speed, hit the armco barrier, performed an airborne spin some ten feet up, hit the barrier again when it came down, and then slithered to a halt in a cloud of dirt and fibreglass. However, the chassis, engine and driver were basically okay, and all of them were back for the next race, albeit after a bit of attention.

The driver now knew that braking whilst out of control at high speed on the grass was basically a bad idea, and the other drivers now knew that they took liberties with a Tuscan at their own risk.

Peter Wheeler has a very good instinctive grasp of what we punters want, and in the Tuscans he was spot on. He told me in as many words in a conversation we had during the first season that he had deliberately made the cars overpowered and undertyred, just to make sure the racing was spectacular. (He also admitted a couple of years later that if he'd known he would be driving the things himself, they would have had 150 BHP and treaded tyres, but he may not have been completely serious.)

Simply making cars fast is not enough. As a motoring writer, it is very rare for me to go motor racing as a spectator. I only ever go club racing, and when the open wheel classes collect on the grid, I wander off in search of a cup of tea. I know they're fast, and plenty of skill and bottle is involved, but for me there's nothing to watch.

On the other hand, historic saloons and sports cars – big old Jags and so on – are hugely entertaining. Lots of whirling of steering wheels, tortured tyres shrieking on the very edge of grip and weighty saloon bodywork swaying around corners in lurid tail slides – big fun. The Tuscans give that level of entertainment, but they're frighteningly fast as well.

If that weren't enough, the kind of people who got involved in the Tuscan series added enormously to the fun. The cars could be bought by anyone at half-price, provided they were raced. This initially meant about £16,000. Half the grid were experienced racing drivers who saw the potential fun in trying to keep these monsters on the track; the rest were rank amateurs who started learning how to drive their cars when the lights went to green. Watching the former trying to keep clear of the latter while still racing each other was almost as much fun for the spectators as it was frustrating for the proper drivers: Gerry Marshall was reduced to gibbering fury on many occasions by learners wandering all over the track – but he still kept coming back for more.

The flavour of the early days of the Tuscan Challenge can be found in a contemporary article I wrote for *Car Builder* magazine:

"It's not that the cars are uncontrollable; Peter Wheeler, TVR's boss, is racing one himself, and his first time out on the racetrack was only last year. Nor

***Early days . . . this is the frantic rush to get all the Tuscans built in time for the start of the racing season.***

is he a youngster; he's bright enough and experienced enough to know his own limitations, and even as a relative novice, the car is forgiving enough – up to a point – to let him put up a respectable showing, even amongst a pretty serious crop of competitors.

The original idea was that the Tuscans should above all else provide good racing. This doesn't necessarily mean just going enormously fast. Airliners go fast, and so do French trains, but they're not any particular fun to watch. Formula One, for me, has a tendency to offer the same lack of fascination, particularly when it takes place on a narrow circuit; if there's only one place to overtake, you can finish up watching a procession of ciggy ads bowling round in the same order for what seems like hours on end, until somebody comes off, or something breaks. Waiting for a breakdown is not top of my list of Fun Stuff To Do.

Having said that, Formula One does have its moments; I think anybody in the world who saw poor old Nigel spluttering to a halt within a few hundred yards of a win must have felt for him. Certainly it must have been politic to keep out of his way for a few days afterwards.

Determined to avoid the possibility of dull racing, TVR made the Tuscans considerably over-powered, as a first priority. Anybody who had the bottle to give a Tuscan its head would automatically be providing the spectators with something to watch.

***Above: The beginning of a race at Brands Hatch: a full grid of Tuscans goes charging up to the hairpin at Druids. Last one to brake is a sissy. Below: The paddock at Brands, with TVR's mobile workshop in the background. This is known as the Bouncy Castle.***

Not content with that, they also made sure the cars were under-tyred as well, just to add to the fun. Over-powered and under-tyred, with almost open headers and racing V8 Rover-based engines? People like Gerry Marshall queuing up to get their hands on the Tuscans? A pretty good formula for seriously entertaining sport, which is in fact what happens.

There was no intention to make the Tuscans easy to drive - rather the opposite if anything – but they've ended up with something of the character of a Cobra; it's relatively easy to make them go pretty fast, but it takes real skill to tread successfully the thin line between going faster than any one else, and overcooking it to finish up in the gravel trap in a cloud of dust.

**Performance Car *magazine's Tuscan taking a wide line at Brands: this may or may not have been a deliberate decision on the part of the driver, John Barker.***

Gerry Marshall's got the hang of the Tuscans. On every straight, it's a point-and-squirt job, with a quick jab on the brakes before the corners (rather later than everyone else) and then a controlled power slide all the way round, just on the ragged edge of breaking away.

Ronnie Farmer, a successful Historic Sports Car driver, usually drives a yellow TVR Griffith, a psychotic little monster from the sixties. This loosely resembles a Turner or Fairthorpe, but packs a full-race American big-block – rather like riding a Scud, in fact. Ronnie usually watches most races from his rear view mirror, and he was impressed with the Tuscan, which is both the direct descendant of the first Griffith, and the forerunnner of the new Griffith, due out this August. The old Griffith and the newer Tuscan share the same sort of subtle-as-a-flying-mallet power, but TVR's handling has apparently improved since 1970.

TVR's boss feels that the amount of power available is absolutely awesome, irrespective of the BHP and mph numbers. The engine is a little stuttery up to about 3000, but from 4000 right up to 8000 the sheer muscle of the thing is tremendous. It's possible to put up a decent showing at Donington, for instance, without changing out of fourth gear, so wide is the band of serious power. The only problem is in deciding how much of it to use; too little and you get elbowed out of the way, too much and you're off.

However, coming off is unlikely to be a serious problem. TVR have been using very solid tubular backbone frames for a long time, and it's unlikely that Peter Wheeler would take the risk of mixing it with the likes of Gerry Marshall unless he was pretty confident of the safety provided by his cars. Certainly my own experience of the Tuscans as a spectator bears this out; I watched one slam head on into a mud bank just feet in front of me, and I really expected to see something fairly unpleasant when the dust cleared. The bonnet had disintegrated, and the impact was hard enough to shake the ground I was standing on.

No worries, however. When the dust cleared, the driver could be seen getting out of the car, swearing at it and kicking it for not going round the corner properly, at the same time holding his thumbs in his armpits because he'd been holding the wheel the wrong way when he hit the bank. A new bonnet frame and radiator, and the same car was hurling itself round the track again at the next meeting in the series.

As far as the spec of the cars goes, you're allowed to modify the springs, shock absorbers, anti-roll bars and airboxes. The rest of the car is supplied by TVR. The engines are not sealed, but are built and almost always rebuilt by the factory themselves. More power wouldn't necessarily make you go much faster, and you'd still have to get past Gerry Marshall anyway.

The engine block is supplied by Rover in a cross-bolted form, and the contents of the crankcase are mostly by TVR themselves, with various goodies lurking inside. The rods are by Carillo, for a start. The engines are tuned and built to go about as fast as they can within the limits of reasonable reliability; with one broken crankshaft in the entire series so far, that seems to have been achieved.

The actual output of the 4.5 litre V8 is 430 BHP at 8000 rpm. The result of this sort of grunt, shoehorned into a relatively light frame covered by a reinforced polyester bodyshell, is an official 0-60 time of 3.6 seconds, with unofficial times nearer 3 seconds flat. 100 mph comes up in four seconds more, and the top speed of 165 mph isn't much further behind.

The suspension on the Tuscans is the traditional TVR independent double wishbones all round,

***Top: The extra bump on the rollcage is an afterthought, to accommodate tall drivers plus their helmets. If you conceive, design, build and race a completely new car in four months, you're entitled to a few*** faux pas. ***Below: In the last ten minutes before a race, things in the paddock have a tendency to become a little fraught.***

supported by coil over shocks; again, most of this is supplied by the factory, but individual owners are at liberty to change shock absorbers and spring rates to suit their own style of driving.

Originally, the Tuscans were to be proven on the track and then released to the general public after a while, but the new Griffith has taken advantage of all the lessons TVR have learned, and has rather elbowed the Tuscan out of the way. One of the Tuscans is road registered and more or less legal, but they are legally only supplied by TVR as pure racetrack cars. I suspect that a few more may find their way on to the road when they've been retired from the race track after a few years, but for the moment, the only way you can get one is if you genuinely intend to thrash its nuts off on the racetrack.

The Tuscan Challenge is seriously good fun to watch; a canvass of people who watched the Birmingham Super Prix in 1990 revealed that they had found the Tuscans more entertaining than the supposed big draw of the Formula 3000 race. Certainly it takes a fair bit to get me off my bum and along to a racetrack as a pure spectator, but the Tuscans have got what it takes.

The rest of the season this year consists of four more races. *Car Builder* will try to make a couple of those meetings, just for the pure fun of watching the

Tuscans roaring and screaming round the track; I suggest you do the same."

The regulations for the Tuscan series have been designed to benefit good drivers over rich drivers, so the allowed changes from the standard spec are minimal. Mind you, when the cars will spin their wheels in fifth gear, it's a moot point as to whether there's much point in making them more powerful.

The actual spec gives the power as 420 BHP at 7750 rpm, and 360 ft/lbs of torque at 5500. The 0-60 time is 3.8 seconds,the 0-100 is 7.6 and the 0-150 mph time is 21.7 seconds. Top speed is 170 mph. As Peter Wheeler has remarked himself, "They're bloody frightening."

***Above: Whoops! One of many 'moments' during the 1993 season. In the wet, with this sort of power available, the difference between enough and too much throttle is not a lot.***

Room for manoeuvre in modifying the engine and drivetrain is minimal. The bore and stroke must be 94mm plus an optional 3 thou, and 80mm plus up to 4 thou. The compression must remain 12.85:1. Valves can only be increased in size by 0.01", and TVR valve springs must be used. The camshaft must be a Kent M256, the pistons Cosworth or TVR and the conrods Carillo or TVR. The crank must be TVR, but having it balanced is permitted.

The crankshafts for the Tuscans actually came from an aborted Leyland project which involved turning the Rover V8 engine into a diesel; they got as far as buying somewhere between six and eight hundred billets of steel, before they decided to use an Italian VM diesel instead of redeveloping the Rover engine. These billets were acquired by TVR as ideal material for making racing crankshafts for the Tuscans.

The carbs are four DRLA48 Dell Orto downdraughts on a TVR inlet manifold. The choice of air filters is free, as is oil cooling and water cooling.

The gearbox has to be the Borg Warner T5, either with standard set ratios or with TVR and Quaife internals. Clutch and cover plate are free, as long as they remain single plate rather than double or triple units. Final drive must be 3.73:1, but the Salisbury 12HU diff, although usually fitted, is not compulsory.

With the suspension wishbones all restricted to TVR manufacture apart from the bushes, the cars can be tuned to suit individual preferences by free choice of damper and spring rates, and by free choice of anti-roll bars as long as they're not adjustable from the cockpit. Seatbelts must be six-point, but are otherwise up to the owner.

The brakes must remain vented four-pot 11.8" discs all round, but variations in brake pad material, brake fluid and master cylinder bores are allowed. The wheels and tyres are restricted to OZ racing split rims, 9" x 16" in size; tyres are Dunlop 210 x 600 x 16. These are slicks; cut slicks are allowed for wet conditions.

The lights must be fully functional, and the battery sealed and leakproof. The weight of the cars must be kept at or above 800 kilograms, their usual weight being about 840 kg, and the exhausts must be standard and must meet RACSMA noise regulations. In 1989, the silencing of the Tuscans was minimal, and the thunder of twenty of them taking off at full throttle was both exhilarating and deafening. Nowadays, the noise levels are a lot more socially acceptable. They still sound glorious, but there's now more orange than vodka in the cocktail of noise.

As far as the bodywork goes, the bootlid can be cut out for access, and extra holes for cooling can be cut by the radiator. Otherwise no more holes can be cut, and no aerodynamic aids are allowed. Extra instruments can be added, and the choice of steering wheel is up to the owner.

It seems a shame that the lines of the Tuscan can't be seen on a road car; but according to TVR, the amount of work that would have been required to bring the design and the moulds up to street standard was pretty well as extensive as designing a whole new car. As a new car was a more interesting prospect, that's the way TVR went.

When the shiny new Fast Lane Tuscan was winched off the trailer, the brothers Dron didn't waste any time in strapping themselves into it. Tony Dron's first impression of the car made it sound very like a Cobra, in that it was wickedly fast on the straight but required very careful handling in corners. Much like the Cobra, the secret of rapid progress was in not upsetting the balance of the car, which responded well to ultra-smooth driving. His overall view of the

***Above: Gerry Marshall's Tuscan, with yet another laurel wreath perched on its windscreen. The forward facing exhausts visible in front of the engine are nearly as big as the air intake pipes. Below: To quote Peter Wheeler: "They're bloody frightening."***

Tuscan came across in one sentence; "... on the start-finish straight I gave it full throttle and discovered that this was the car I'd always wanted".

Brother Peter was visibly respectful of the Tuscan, as the car had given him a verbal warning by spinning spectacularly without much provocation. "Basically the car is an animal," he mused. "It tells you you've got things slightly wrong by swapping ends several times."

Part of the sheer fun of the Tuscan series came across when an experienced racing driver came fresh from setting a lap record in a 500 BHP Sierra. "No fun at all compared to a Tuscan drive," he said. This was despite experiencing the familiar sphincter-clenching party trick of the early Tuscans which involved a pipe coming off the fuel system and spraying petrol all over the red hot manifold, resulting in undignified exits from the track amid sheets of flame. Unwise to use all the brakes at once, he recommended, before describing the Tuscan Challenge as "the rugby of motor sports", obviously wondering if there was a team anywhere looking for members.

John Barker, talking about the *Performance Car*/BP sponsored Tuscan, remarked that "the Tuscans lap as quickly as the faster single-seaters, and their handling isn't what I'd call benign." His comment about his forearms being 'pumped up like Red Rum's thighs' as he tried to keep a grip on the kicking, shuddering steering wheel under braking, is echoed by Ryan Baptiste. "Bowel-loosening tail slides and arm-stiffening weaves under braking ..."

Barker can have the last word, which may go some way to getting an idea of the pure fun involved; "The in-gear acceleration times are, quite frankly, ludicrous."

*Left: Scrutineered, twitching and queueing up for the start line. The adrenalin is pumping, with good cause. Below: I can see the economics of it, but I still think it's a shame that the gorgeous Tuscan lines can't be seen on the road.*

# Chapter 7

# Twenty Years of Production

***Mike Penny – TVR's production guru for the last twenty years.***

Production at TVR has been quietly and steadily developing over the years under the direction of Mike Penny. As it stands at the moment, there are no cars held in stock, and there haven't been any since the company has been riding its current wave of popularity.

There is now a wait of about three or four months for a car, and there is no discount offered. There's no need, when a secondhand Griffith costs more than a new one; the last secondhand Griff that became available at the factory had four TVR dealers scrambling over each other to pay over the odds for it. However, there is no complacency at TVR; they are well aware that there are discount bargains to be had from Porsche and the like, and that there is a limit to the amount of patience that they can expect from their customers in a buyers' market.

The short initial production run of the Griffith, followed by a hiatus while the Chimaera took priority, sent the desirability and secondhand price of the Griff through the roof, but it wasn't a marketing stunt. (Although if it had been, it would have been a very good one.) It's simply that even with a permanent night shift, TVR can only produce about 17 cars a week. They could go for more volume, but only at the expense of the very nature of TVR cars. The company is doing well at the moment, so it seems silly to change the basic idea, particularly when they have a pretty good idea of why they're doing so well.

One wonders what John Harvey Jones would see if he looked at TVR; his evaluation of Morgan was fascinating for the way it largely missed the point. People don't object to being on the waiting list for years; that's part of what they're buying. Certainly, an ancient and odd production methodology is applied in the fact of commercial logic, but the fact that the chaps are happy building it that way is enough of a reason to carry on doing it the same way for another sixty years. There's also the point that a Morgan is a new but still genuinely vintage car, and if the plant or the car were modernised, that would be lost. Is there much of that sort of anachronistic approach at TVR?

No, not really. There is a certain amount of flying in the face of conventional wisdom, but that's mostly a matter of clarity of vision; production methods at TVR are certainly old-fashioned, but only where that's the best way of doing the job. The basic format of the cars is also old-fashioned, but that's just a coincidence. If front wheel drive were fast as well as being cheap to

*Above: The Chimaera has a much less aggressive look than the Griff: unless you knew, you would be very surprised to find that the two cars shared a chassis. Left: The fat haunches of the Griffith follow the sweeping line from the front of the car: muscle and curves incarnate.*

***The Chimaera shape is more restrained than the sleekly beautiful Griffith: it's more of a grand tourer than a pure sports car.***

Eighties. The fashion changes which saw the sharp, classic lines of the Audi Quattro Coupe deteriorating into the squat, graceless lump of the later Audi Coupe were concurrent with the development of the Tasmin's razor edges into the muscles and curves of the 420 shapes.

In the case of the TVR, the basic well-balanced shape was retained, and the curves simply made an already attractive shape look smoother and more aggressive at the same time.

However, gorgeous though the lines of the old 420 were, it was still an old design revamped: it was time for Wheeler to begin to make his mark on the company with new cars. The basic idea behind the TVR was in no real need of any change. The design team, as ever, were brimming over with sexy new ideas for screaming turbo engines, rear-engined Ferrari thrashers and all sorts of innovations, but none of them had come up with any new information that would change Peter's mind about the basic format of the cars.

Rear mid in-line engines are certainly the best format for open wheeled single seater racing cars, and Peter will happily endorse that philosophy – for single seater racing cars. However, there's no reason why that format should be good for fast two seater road cars. I've now driven a Pontiac Fiero with a rear mid transverse engine for some time, and I can endorse Peter's view in various ways. Whether the overall dynamics of rear engined road cars make them slightly faster, I don't know. They make me personally slower, because I'm conscious that my ankles are the first line of defence. If I hit anything, I am between the engine and the object, which is an uncomfortable feeling. We have all experienced this phenomenon already, of course: if your thumb gets between a hammer and a nail, it hurts. In practical terms for road use, rear mid engine fitment is silly. The boot space is pathetic, the wheel arches take up half the cabin and still aren't wide enough to give the car a usable steering lock, there are an extra fifty feet or so of radiator hoses and throttle cables to give problems, engine access is appalling and the gearbox is even

# Chapter 9
# Building a Griff

Although the Griffith and the Chimaera are worlds apart from the Vixens of the Sixties, they are still built basically the same way. It's rather like the difference between listening to Cream on a boosted 8-track tape machine in a manky old Triumph Vitesse, and listening to Kiri Te Kanawa on digital tape in an anechoic hi-fi showroom; they're both basically singing songs, but one of them is rather more sophisticated. On the other hand, they're both worth listening to. (I promised not to mention Kylie Minogue, so I won't.)

These are still very much hand-made cars. Something like six hundred hours of labour goes into each TVR, and between 70% and 80% of the car is made at the factory; the springs, shocks, brakes, steering racks and gearboxes are bought in, but most of the rest of the car is either made at the factory or radically altered at TVR Power in Coventry.

The Griffith in question starts life in the chassis shop as a collection of lengths of round and square steel tubing with the odd piece of sheet metal for brackets, and on the other side of the factory as rolls of GRP matting and a drum of resinous goop. Not very glamorous at this stage, I'm afraid.

The steel tubing is cut to length and assembled on jigs into three chassis sections. Each section is completed on its own small jig, and is fitted with all the brackets for the suspension, the component mountings and so on. This allows minor changes to be made to each of the front and rear sections, which

***The chassis welding boys. The general atmosphere on the shop floor at TVR is pretty good, with everyone cheerfully charging about building cars as fast as they can, and taking the piss out of writers if they come within range.***

***Top: The front end of the Griffith/Chimaera chassis. Brackets on the left and right are for the wishbones, the central one is for the coilover shock. Above: The rear end of the chassis, with all its bracing bars combining to form a rigid cage for the differential. Right: The front and back ends of the chassis are welded to the centre section, which allows quick and convenient changes to accommodate building the longer Cerbera chassis.***

carry the suspension components, without putting the whole jig out of action.

If you do this welding-together business with tinplate monocoque cars, you are liable to have earnest BBC types from Watchdog breathing down your neck, or you may even have to give Roger Cook a thump. Welding together bits of damaged biscuit tin does carry a risk for their subsequent drivers, but with the sort of chassis you find under a TVR, the practice is demonstrably completely safe. On several occasions, I've seen people walk away uninjured from racetrack prangs in TVRs that they would have had to be cut out of if the cars had been pressed steel monocoques. If I have a biggy at any stage, I do hope I'm in a car with a proper chassis and a thick GRP body when it happens.

When the front and rear chassis sections are complete, they are welded on to the centre section, which is built and then held in place on a much larger jig. This methodology proved convenient recently, when a jig had to be made for the extended Cerbera chassis. All they had to do was to make a new jig for the centre section, as the front and back sections remain standard and are welded on later.

The new jig for the Cerbera centre section wasn't simply a cut and shut job, however, as the torsional rigidity with the longer tubes was lower than the shorter original Chimaera chassis. However, with a little judicious stiffening at key points it was soon up to the required stiffness.

When the centre part of the chassis of the Griff in question has been assembled and its front and back have been welded on, the whole assembly is then upended for the other side to be welded. At the same time, while some parts are laser cut by a subcontractor, most of the numerous thick sheet steel brackets and mountings are being cut, shaped and trimmed in another part of the factory.

The process of shipping steel in and forming it into various Griffith components is a continuous system that runs as smoothly as it can; Mike Penny as production director has to perform the delicate balancing trick of making sure there's no danger of running out, while at the same time keeping the amount of stockpiled steel as small as possible to keep the costs down.

A new sight at TVR is a stash of sheet aluminium; wherever possible, manufacturing of the cars is being brought in-house, and the sheet aluminium in question is now used for making petrol tanks. As well as keeping the costs under control, you can solve any production problems far more quickly when you can simply walk across the factory and talk to the person who's making the tanks.

When the Griff chassis is complete, it's taken along to the powder coating plant. This is essentially a

*Top left: The powder coating oven has a slow moving overhead conveyor belt. Left: Steel components manufactured at TVR, such as the suspension wishbones pictured, are hooked on to the conveyor belt for their trip through the oven. Top right: The whole chassis is also coated in epoxy powder and passed through the same process: here a pile of finished chassis are awaiting transfer to the rolling chassis building area. Below: The steering and suspension parts are fitted to the chassis in its next step towards completion.*

*Right: The completed front end of the chassis, showing the suspension, hubs and anti-roll bar. The steering rack is still to be fitted. Below: The assembled rear end, with the diff and fluid lines all fitted. The old aluminium uprights from Vixen days are now fabricated steel items with no unpleasant surprises in store for the enthusiastic driver.*

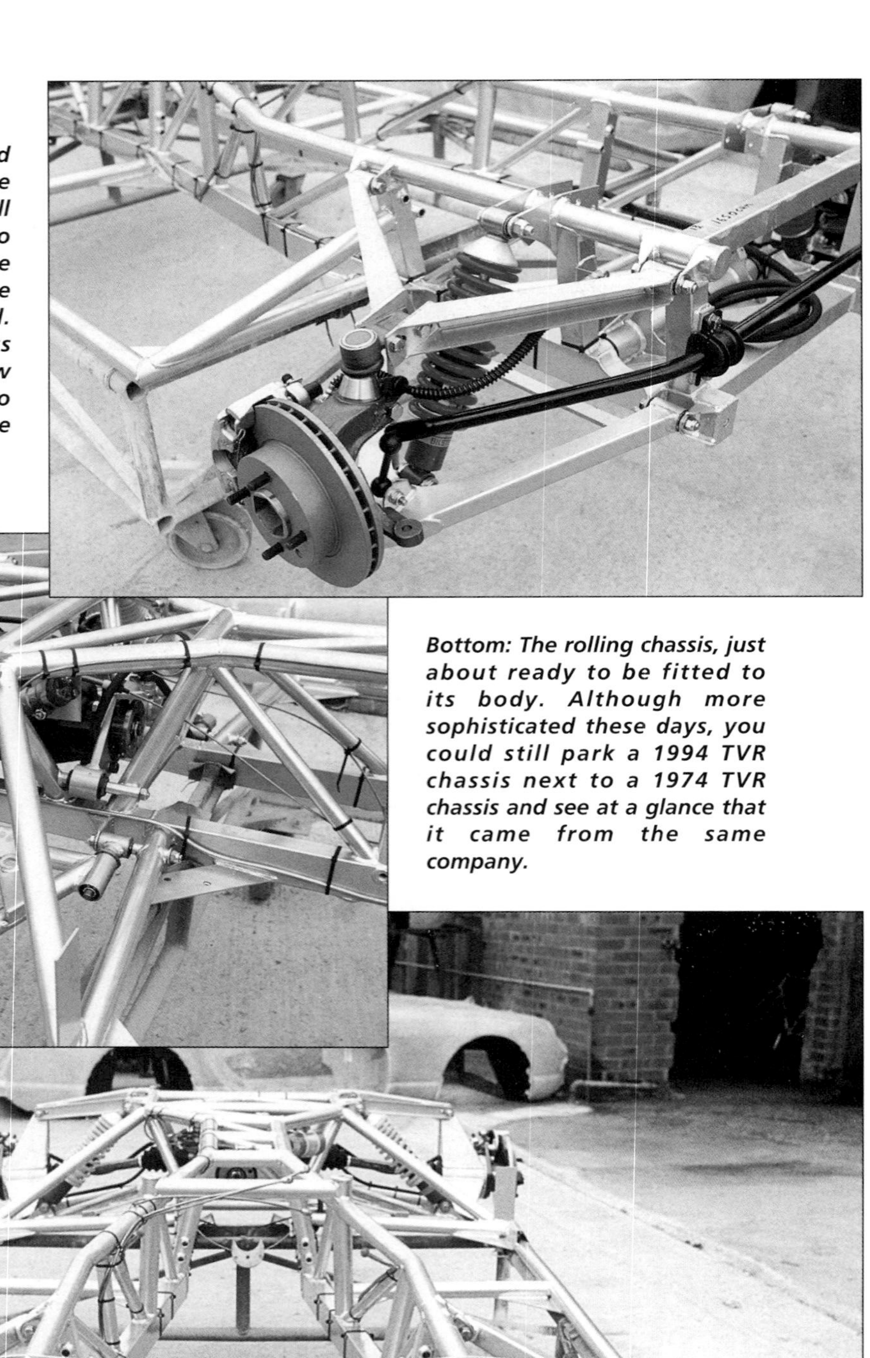

*Bottom: The rolling chassis, just about ready to be fitted to its body. Although more sophisticated these days, you could still park a 1994 TVR chassis next to a 1974 TVR chassis and see at a glance that it came from the same company.*

*Top: Into the moulding shop: the shape of the car can be seen in the body mould, braced with steel to keep it in shape. The bodies are still laid up by hand: for small volumes, it's still the best way. Right: The bodies are trimmed. The moulding lines that result from the joins in the mould are nearly all hidden inside panels on the TVRs, to keep wasted time and motion to a minimum.*

*Left: The finished Griffith body is mounted on its chassis and rolled off to the paint shop. Below: The bodywork is rubbed down painstakingly by hand, primed and rubbed down again. The only way to get a really good finish on a GRP body is by sheer hard work.*

*Left: The doors, bootlids and bonnets are prepped and painted separately, although they all go through the same long process of finishing. Top: Painted doors, previously trimmed and shaped to fit their own particular body and then fitted with the wiring for their mirrors and window motors, sit on a rack awaiting their cars.*

*Right: The two-pack paint job of up to twelve coats is tough, long-lasting and very shiny indeed. Bottom left: The main assembly area, where the painted body/chassis units are fitted out with the rest of their componentry. Bottom right: TVR now make their own welded aluminium fuel tanks: as much of the manufacturing process as possible is gradually being brought in-house for economy and control.*

long, high cooker with a big suspended cable running through it. The epoxy coating is applied with an ordinary paint shop spray gun, and the chassis is then hooked up on to the line. When the line is started, the chassis moves slowly along the interior of the cooker, and by the time it emerges from the other end, it's as crisp and tasty as anyone could ask. All the TVR-made suspension components, and in fact any steel bits likely to suffer from corrosion, are also powder coated.

After the powder room, the chassis goes to the chassis build up area, where the suspension, springs, anti-roll bar, steering and differential are fitted. The brakes, the fuel and hydraulic lines are also plumbed in at this stage, and the resultant almost-rolling chassis is

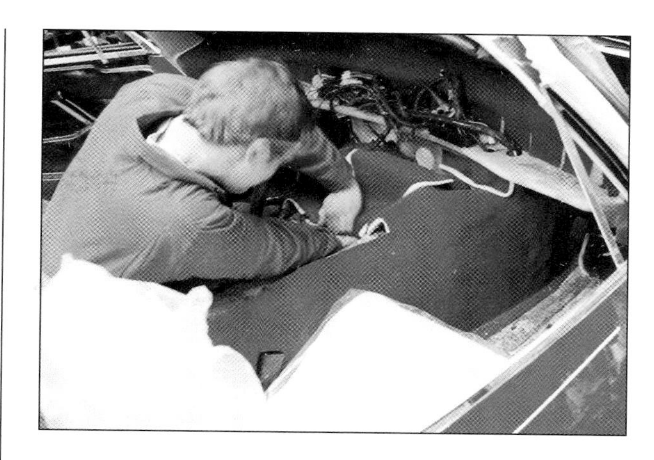

hefted up on to one of dozens of little wheeled bogies and is rolled through to the body shop to be fitted with its bodyshell. Concurrently with the chassis, the Griffith's body has been under construction at the other end of the plant. The body shell is made in one large lump, rather than being a collection of disparate sections. The main tub, the transmission tunnel, the floors and all four wings are moulded together as one large item. This has various advantages. Mainly it results in a better car dynamically. The stiffer the structure, the better the handling, so if you fit a stiff body to an already stonking chassis, the whole car benefits; this is particularly important for convertibles. Have a look under a convertible conversion of a monocoque production car, and you'll see much welded-on evidence of an attempt to put some sort of rigidity back into a structure that's essentially as floppy as a dunked Hobnob.

In a small factory which is already crowded, there are also practical production advantages in one-piece construction. The less moulds and bits you have around the better. Also, making the whole thing in one piece means you don't have to waste time making it fit together afterwards, and generally saves time and keeps costs down.

There aren't really any disadvantages to this method of body construction; if you prang one corner of a Griff, the repair involves cutting out the damaged bit and bonding a new section in. Repairing GRP bodywork is relatively quick and easy; I'm as cack-handed as they come, and even as a total amateur I was able to repair a seriously damaged GRP bodyshell so that you couldn't see the joins. Even if for instance the front end were separate like the old Taimars and the current Tuscan, it would probably be about as cheap to repair the panel in situ as to replace it. Ever

***Left: The TVR manufactured pedal box is fitted with proprietary components, before the complete assembly goes into the car. Top: Fitting the carpeting and trim. In the same way as the making of the leather dashboards, the skills involved in doing this can't be duplicated by machines. Bottom: The dashboard wiring looks rather terrifying, but is actually simpler than it looks. Each collection of coloured tagliatelle finishes up in a simple plug. At least, that's how the theory goes.***

mindful of the fact that hard-driven Griffiths may occasionally come a cropper, TVR run up a proportion of extra bodyshells; if you have a little misunderstanding, you can buy replacement bodywork by the foot.

The body itself is laid up by hand. The moulds are polished before each body is made, as careful preparation at this stage saves time and hassle correcting imperfections later. The hard, shiny outer gelcoat is painted into the moulds first, then the glassfibre matting is rolled on, with the polyester resin stippled and rolled into it. The floor panel is the first to be laid up, followed by the body sides and then the smaller sections. The number of layers of matting

***Top: The organic shape of the dashboard is covered in foam and then the leather is carefully tightened over it and clipped and glued in place. Bottom: All we need now is an engine and box... Right: The TVR Power version of Rover's ubiquitous aluminium V8, with the manifolds swept forwards to the main catalytic convertor.***

applied to different areas varies, according to where the extra strength is most needed.

When the resin has partly hardened, the edges are trimmed to shape, and prepared with more resin and matting where the sections join together; the sections of the moulds are then bolted together. The whole assembly is then left overnight, which sets up the GRP fairly solidly.

The next day, the bodyshell is broken out of the mould and taken to the first stages of body preparation. First the whole thing is turned upside down for the flashlines to be ground off. Flashlines are raised lines of surplus GRP left over at the places where the moulds bolt together. When the underside of the Griffith's body is in good shape, it's turned the right way up again, and fitted onto its chassis.

At this point the serious graft starts. The holes for the lights and so on are cut out and trimmed, and then each square inch of the body work is rubbed down to a matt finish by hand, and any tiny imperfections in the finish are filled. Anyone who has done any of this sort of work on GRP bodies won't be surprised to learn that most people who work in that area of TVR have worn their fingerprints completely off.

When the base finish looks spot on, the body, now bolted down to the chassis, is rolled through to the curing ovens, where it is cooked for four to five hours at 65-70 degrees centigrade. This brings any latent imperfections in the GRP to the surface where they can be dealt with, and also relieves any stresses that may have built up in the bodyshell. When the Griffith cools down after removal from the oven, the chassis and body fit perfectly.

The doors, boot and bonnet don't fit at this stage, however. They're oversize when they're made, and they are then hinged to the individual bodyshell, and trimmed and adjusted to fit. While people seem quite happy to accept yawning gaps on production cars, they always complain about gaps on GRP cars; the TVR approach to this is to give them nothing to winge about in the first place. The doors, boot and bonnet are therefore treated with particular concentration until they fit perfectly, then they're marked up with numbers to identify them as the panels for that particular body, and removed to be sprayed separately.

The main bodyshell, meanwhile, has moved on to be jet washed to get rid of all the fibreglass dust, and the body is sprayed in its first coat of primer. It's then baked for thirty minutes to harden the paint, and rubbed down by hand. The second coat is then applied, baked and rubbed down. Then the third and

***Top: The engine with its gearbox fitted is swung over the engine bay on a hoist and carefully lowered into place. By the time TVR Power have finished with the V8, it's rather more convincing than the standard Rover item. Bottom: The V8, in this case a 4.3, fits neatly into the Griff's engine bay. Padded wing covers protect the paintwork from scratches.***

***Top: Up on to the overhead ramp, for final fitting out and the assembly of the exhaust system aft of the main bucket-sized catalytic convertor. Above: At the other end of the ramp, the Griff is started up for the first time, then the engine is tuned up and it's off to pre-delivery inspection.***

fourth coats; not many fingerprints left in this department either. The bodyshell ultimately finishes up as smooth as Bryan Ferry, at which point it's ready for some serious paint.

The topcoat spray booth is heated to 50 degrees centigrade, and the number of layers of paint needed varies according to the type of finish ordered. Flat colour gets five coats, most metallics get about eight, and pearlescent finishes get twelve coats altogether. The Griff is now rolled out of the booth and is left alone for 24 hours until the two-pack finish has cured to its final rock hard gloss.

The doors, bonnet and boot have all been going through the same process, and they are now collected and fitted to the bodyshell. The chassis is fitted with its wheels and lifted off its little bogie, which goes off back to the beginning to carry another emerging car. The Griff is rolled through to be fitted with its tank, filler neck, pedal box and radiator, and then moves on to door fitting, where the windows, window motors and door wiring looms go in.

The wiper motor, heater, fuel sender and so on are next, at which point the car is ready to be fitted with its wiring loom. This is another item made entirely in-house. There are racks of dozens of rolls of different colours and thicknesses of wire, and the looms are constructed by the time-honoured and reliable method of a big board with lots of nails in it. When each wire has been run along its allotted path on the peg board, the whole thing is wrapped in tape, and various smaller components are attached to the loom. It is then fitted to the car and clipped in place. Old fashioned, yes, but anyone who has ever tried to get the high tech imprinted banding system working on a Cortina dash will welcome the prospect of proper wires and proper old-fashioned contacts.

With the loom in place, the interior and the boot of the car are carpeted. Still rolling on its wheels along the factory floor, the car is next fitted with the upper and lower parts of the steering column, the seat belts, the door seals, the windscreen and surround, and the wipers and washer system. The bonnet is fitted and adjusted,and the hood rail, hoop and roof panel are fitted and trimmed. The neat little twist grip on the transmission tunnel that opens the doors is connected to its cables.

Now heading strongly for the overhead ramp and completion, the car is fitted with its engine and gearbox, gearlinkage and gear lever. The engines arrive from TVR Power in Coventry having been built as ordered for each car, according to what the owner wants. Big bore, dustbin sized valves, whatever. Perhaps it's something of a clue to the nature of the owners to reflect that there has as yet been no Griffith built with a 'standard' 4-litre engine.

The battery and cables go in next, with the fuel system, the alarm, and the dashboard. The engine is wired up to the electrical system, all the electrics so far fitted are now tested, and the headlamp beams are adjusted. The trimming of the interior is another matter handled in-house, and if full leather seems an expensive option, prospective owners can comfort themselves with the thought that there's very little profit in it for TVR by the time they've finished a full hide interior. Leather that's good enough to look the business and that's also tough enough to withstand being used in a car does not come cheap.

The glorious, organic curves in the leather Griffith dashboard are achieved by making a swoopy GRP moulding from the same material as the body. This is then padded with a thin layer of soft plastic foam, and the whole assembly is covered with a very carefully cut and hand-stitched sheet of tanned and dyed leather, which is gently stretched over the whole panel and then glued in place. There's no short cut; it just takes years of practice and seriously expensive leather to achieve the sort of finish you see in a Griff. With the interior sorted out, the ramp beckons, and the Griffith is pushed up on to it. Door internals are trimmed, the door speakers, cigar lighter and electric mirror controls are fitted and connected, and the propshaft and exhaust system are fitted underneath, by a cheerful crew with permanently stiff necks. The exhausts are a bit of a novelty, in that the manifolds or headers point forwards and collect in a can the size of a pedal bin, which contains a catalytic convertor; they then sweep back under the car through two more cats to exit as a twin system from under the tail. Finally, assorted fuel and air widgetry is fitted, all the suspension bushes are tightened up to the correct torque, and every nut and bolt under the car is checked for tightness. The steering and suspension geometry is adjusted and set, the various engine and gearbox oils and fluids are added, and the brakes are filled with brake fluid, bled and adjusted. Almost finished now, the car is wheeled off the ramp and started up for the first time. The timing and carbon dioxide emission are set, and the car moves for the first time under its own power, round to the next section for its pre-delivery inspection.

Once it has been given a good going over by the PDI boys, it is taken for a test drive by one of the company's directors. When he is happy that everything is working perfectly, the car is valeted, polished and delivered to the dealer or importer.

***...and another gorgeous Griffith hits the road.***

## Chapter 10

# Driving a Chimaera

A tough job this, but someone had to do it. Having spent a morning topping up my collection of factory floor shots, rearranging grubby bits of chassis and so on to get decent pictures of how they're built, the afternoon was due to be spent in the company of TVR's brand new press officer and Tuscan Challenge co-ordinator, one Ben Samuelson.

An extremely jammy chap, Ben. An ardent TVR enthusiast, he spent a considerable portion of his penultimate year at Edinburgh University pestering Peter Wheeler with letters and phone calls until Wheeler capitulated and gave him the summer job he'd been hassling for. Having got it, he soon found himself making a useful contribution as a copywriter, although a tendency to floridity in his writing style had

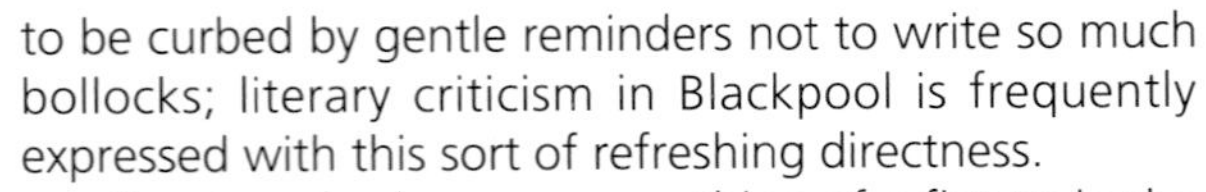

to be curbed by gentle reminders not to write so much bollocks; literary criticism in Blackpool is frequently expressed with this sort of refreshing directness.

Ben has also become something of a fixture in the hospitality tent at the Tuscan Challenge races, making sure that everybody knows everybody else, and keeping the gentlemen of the press well stocked with propaganda and gin. The sporting of slightly noisy young-fogey waistcoats and a habitual air of cheerful gregariousness livens things up too.

Then came an unlikely and enviable piece of luck. James Pillar, TVR's press officer and race co-ordinator, who had been doing an excellent job keeping TVR on the front pages of every motoring magazine in the country, had in fact done such a noticeably good job that he was poached. Did Ben fancy abandoning his history degree to take over when James left? Not many. After all, he could already produce a convincing Morningside *eccent*, which is *efter oll* the major purpose of getting a degree from Edinburgh ... so the Athens of the North got the elbow as soon as the bright lights of Blackpool beckoned.

***The author looking pleased with himself, as well he might: most people have to work for a living, and it's only a lucky few who get to charge around the place in fab cars and call it work.***

On my Chinaera day, all this had just happened, and Ben was still beside himself with unrestrained glee as he approached his second task as press officer elect, which was to accompany your narrator on an afternoon's blast on the country roads.

Red, was the Chimaera in question, and absolutely mint. It sat there in the car park behind the factory looking big, new and undeniably red. The overall shape is less radical than the Griffith, and the radiator grille offers you a cheery grin rather than the serious expression of the Griffith.

The chopped sculptings down the sills are apparently quite genuinely the result of a spot of creative interference by Peter's unruly and aerobic dog Ned. There being a dearth of bones in the office, Ned had a bit of a chew at

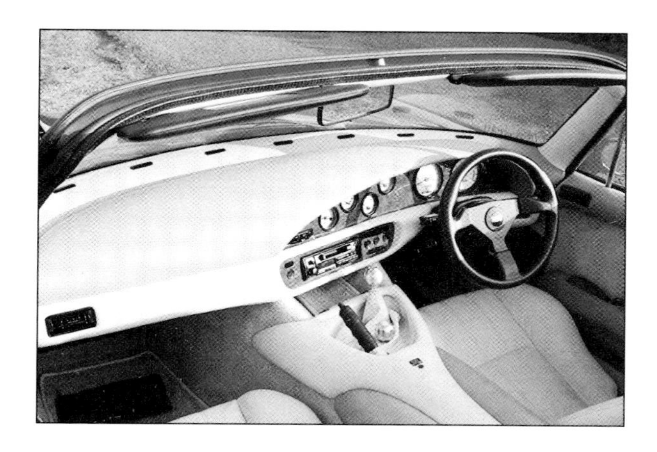

the original small model of the Chimaera, which at that moment was code-named Ugly Pig 1. The toothmarks became sculpted lines, and these in the finished car add an element of originality to a design that otherwise might have been just quite attractive.

Anyway, having admired the shiny red beast for a bit, we ambled over towards it. "The usual routine is that I drive for a bit first, then you get to play with it," said Ben.

Fair enough, I thought. After all, one doesn't want to risk performing a lurid fishtail start in front of several dozen observers, particularly when there is no formal policy on not taking the piss out of writers.

I went round the back to put my camera bag and tripod in the boot. Ah. No sign of any handles, keyholes or anything of that ilk; the bootlid lock is electric and remote. You have to turn on the ignition and press a button under the dash. Buzz plop, it went, and I opened the lid.

Ben squinted up at the sun. "Shall we have the roof off?" he asked.

"Silly question, really," I replied.

"Yes, I suppose it was."

The roof is a very simple and elegant design. In fact, when you look at it, you wonder why all convertibles aren't designed that way. Rather than a canvas affair, the central section is a rigid Kevlar panel, which locks into the top of the windscreen frame. Then the rear section, which involves a bit of canvas and a bendy plastic window, hinges up to meet the back of the Kevlar roof panel. Two thick aluminium bars with sort of knees in the middle then snap into place, and you've virtually got a hardtop on in about ten seconds.

The roof comes off in the same sort of time, and the roof panel is stowed in the boot, which is a reasonably good size, even with the panel taking up a fair bit of room. Lots of room for my ratty old bag and tripod, anyway. The only criticism I would make is that the rear section doesn't fold down far enough, which makes it difficult to see over the top of it when you're reversing.

***Left: The snug and inviting cockpit. The blend of ultramodern organic curves and the wood and leather of a traditional gentleman's sports car works very well. Below: All sorts of subtle curves and shapes are apparent in the Chimaera body looked at through a long lens. Even without the dog tooth detailing, the body line would still have been distinctive.***

The seats are snug, and they make you take up a relaxed position whether you're feeling relaxed or not. At the moment I drive an Eagle jeep, in which you sit upright like a truck driver, with acres of room around you in every direction. The TVR interior is far more purposeful than that, and you sort of plop into a human-sized slot in it, as if it had been made for you.

***Below: The Chimaera greets you with a cheery grin rather than the slightly psychotic pout of the Griffith. The Chimaera is actually more amiable in character, although it's nearly as fast as the Griff across country. Bottom: Up at the business end of the car, the 4.3 litre V8 nestles well back in the engine bay. The huge exhaust header pipes meet in the middle, where the first bucket sized catalyst is located.***

A very welcoming feeling, actually. Although the dashboard rather excludes the passenger from the conversation; the dash only talks to the driver, and the passenger is ignored, once inserted and strapped in. This car is only interested in drivers.

"There's a place called the something of something that might be good for pictures," said Ben. "Shall we give that a try?"

"It sounds irresistible to me," I replied. "The what of what?"

"The Trough of something or other, I think. It's over towards the Lakes."

The starter struggled briefly against the compression of the engine for a second or two until it burst into life, rising in note for a few seconds until it settled into the usual slightly rough TVR chumbling. This is something I've noticed before – TVR engines never just start up like ordinary boring engines. They always wind themselves up and then explode into life. This even applies to elderly and wrinkled ones like Vixens, with Cortina engines in them. There's always a bit of drama involved.

Out of the grubby concrete area round the back of the factory, and through the suburbs of Blackpool, heading East towards the open road. A brief open space appears, and Ben changes down a gear and opens the throttle. A snarl from behind, and the red Chimaera leaps forward, then calms down as the traffic clutters up again.

"I can't believe I'm actually getting paid to do this," said Ben. Certainly, for an individual who is naturally hospitable and also fanatical about TVRs, to get a job which involves both playing with them and telling people about them is unbelievable luck. However, the universe will undoubtedly exact some sort of retribution sooner or later. He's bound to fall in love with a girl who doesn't like sex, or to get leprosy or bilharzia or something. Nobody gets that lucky and gets away with it.

However, having cheerfully agreed that divine retribution was on its way sooner or later, we decided to hope it wouldn't be meted out today, and concentrated on the sunshine and the glorious chords of the Chimaera's exhaust note.

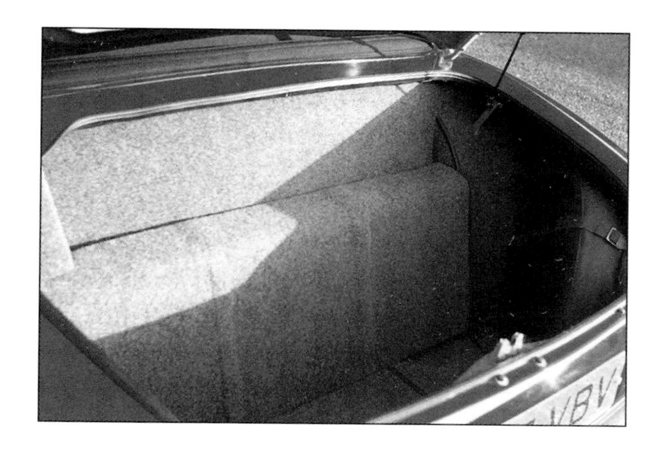

The countryside unwound itself through the windscreen, and I noticed that the car remained pretty civilised in spite of the top being off. Conversation was possible even at relatively high speeds, even if it was inconsequential drivel and probably not worth listening to. There wasn't any battering from the slipstream either. When you go for a long blast in a Cobra replica, you generally finish up knackered and temporarily deafened. None of that with the Chimaera; partly, I think, because you are in it rather than on it. The big sweepy windscreen and the half-folded rear section probably help too.

"Stop stop stop!" I said, having spotted a potential photo location, a vista involving the sun glistening off extensive mud flats. The car stopped, and I got out and had a look. Actually, it wasn't really a tasty view at all, it just looked good compared with the bum end of Blackpool.

The keys flashed in an arc through the air. "Your turn," said Ben, strapping himself into the passenger seat. "Don't for God's sake prang it, or it's back to A.J.P. Taylor and The Origins of the First World War for me."

"Yum yum," I thought to myself, thumbing the door button, opening the door and plopping into the pilot's seat. This is by far the more entertaining side of the car. You are held firmly in precisely the right place, and the organic sweep of the veneered dash presents you with all the information you need, right where you want it. The whole cockpit fitted me so well that the position of the steering wheel, by comparison, felt decidedly odd; however, it turned out to be adjustable, so I messed about with it until it was precisely where I wanted it.

Poke the loud pedal and twist the key, churr churr churr woomph. The car twitches with the torque of the engine, and I push the stubby gear lever into first. The clutch is of medium weight, but the steering feels like the wheels are set in concrete until you get going. Like my own Cobra replica, you can barely move the wheel when the car's stationary. The Chimaera's the same; you learn not to try turning the steering wheel until the car is moving. As soon as it's under way, however, the steering comes to life.

Power steering is on the way for these cars, I understand; for a car that is so effectively a dual-

***Left: The boot on the Chimaera is a good bit bigger than that of the Griffith. Even with the Kevlar roof panel in the boot, there's plenty of space for a weekend's luggage. Below: This is what the view from the office looks like. Words can't tell you what it feels like, but if you imagine being licked all over by a diminutive Australian sex goddess, it's probably about half as good as that.***

purpose performance toy and practical usable transport, it will be a boon. Driving it is great, parking it is hard going. Provided that the power steering can be restricted to very low speeds to keep the feel of the steering at speed just the way it is, it will answer my only reservation about the dynamic performance of the car.

I was taught to treat very powerful cars with considerable respect by a Cobra that once tried to kill me. The dry mouth, the ticking, stalled engine and the thick curly black lines of rubber stretching across the road as I gazed down the long bonnet at my own even longer skidmarks form a picture I recall to mind whenever I'm tempted to push my luck.

The Chimaera certainly provided no end of temptation. As soon as you get rolling, there is an immediate feeling of security and stability, as well as the barely concealed power that also makes itself felt.

The roads emptied as the country deepened, and I got to know the car a little better, giving it more throttle and using the brakes a little harder. The handling felt absolutely safe and predictable. I usually drive very circumspectly until I feel familiar enough with a car to take any liberties, but in the Chimaera I felt at home within a couple of miles.

A few long smooth corners, and a bit more throttle; the car sits absolutely solid on its line, although the steering is so sensitive you can feel each bump, each line and each discarded dog-end on the road surface. A Jag in front suddenly sees the Chimaera's cheerful grille grinning in his mirror. He's going quite quickly, and decides to be obstructive. However, there's lots of room, there's nobody else about, and I'm driving a very serious car indeed. I indicate, pull out, change into third and boot it. There is a howl from the exhausts, and I hit the back of my seat as the Chimaera's rear end squats minimally, then we hurtle forward, the Jag whips past the offside window and dwindles in the mirror.

***With the windows up and the hood folded down halfway, which is as far as it will go, the airstream mostly goes over the cockpit, making high speed cruising a pretty civilised business.***

Up to fourth, scenery blurring, then fifth, then the crest of a hill looms up. Blip fourth, brake, blip blip third, brake a bit harder, no sign of fade or any objection from the suspension, a lightness over the top of the crest then a thud on the suspension as our weight comes down. Again, not a twitch. The suspension on this car is so well sorted, it's not true. Back on the throttle and we're off again, sweepy corners, narrow bits. A hundred yards of clear road, boot it, the needles dance round the rev counter and the speedo, back on the brakes, clawing it down hard for the next corner, and I know from experience that I have still not taken this car to even fifty percent of its abilities.

It's superb; it is a real thoroughbred. I can think of a few cars that have given me a similar visceral buzz, but not many. My favourite drives have included a Dax Tojeiro with a seven-litre high performance big-block V8 in it, a tiny, delicate and wicked JZR replica of a 1928 Morgan trike, powered by a motorcycle engine that revved to twelve thousand, and a genuine 1936 Jaguar SS100. Blattering through empty countryside in a real pre-war thoroughbred that was still bloody fast despite its age was definitely a high point, but I'd say this TVR is very definitely up there with the all time favourites.

"Stop stop stop!" said Ben; I glanced in the mirror and then stamped on the anchors. We both hit the straps as the car came to a very rapid but drama-free stop.

"That sign back there, the Trough of Bowland, that's what we're looking for."

"The Slough of Despond, hey?" I smirked. As a fellow pseudo-literate smartarse, I can expect Ben either to be familiar with the odd literary reference, or at least to be embarrassed enough by his ignorance to pretend he's familiar with it, which comes to much the same thing.

Stretching my neck to see over the hood, I backed up, and we went wandering off down a side road. The terrain got lumpier, and suddenly we popped over a little crest, and a sort of lost valley appeared.

"Ey up, this is a bit fab, isn't it?" I said. Miles of rolling blue hills, rocky streams and a winding little road ambling between them. Yowl yowl yowl came from behind, and a huge fat fluorescent motorcycle shot by, with a small fluorescent rider perched atop it. Another even fatter

*The Turbo. Not the most subtle of cars to start with, and the extremely red leather interior does nothing to tone down the general effect. Great fun and very fast.*

TVR
390 SE

*Opposite: the long nose of a 390SE stretches back to some of the other current options. A blast of TVRs? A wedge? A rage? Above: Muscle and curves begin to appear in the 390SE. The engine is now considerably improved, and a distinct waist is beginning to appear in the body. Left: TVR100 again, this time on a 420SE.*

***Two examples of the 420SEAC. "420" meant that the 3.5 litre V8 was now bored out to 4.2 litres as well as having been seriously interfered with: "SEAC" meant Special Equipment Aramid Composite, i.e. a lightweight Kevlar body. The SEAC's wild tea tray and even wilder performance showed the competition how it should be done.***

*Left: The ubiquitous light alloy Rover V8, which TVR have now been using and abusing for more than a decade. Below: this is the future. TVR's own engine is now doing even better than expected in trials in a racing car, and will shortly begin road trials.*

*The Chimaera appeals to the more mature sports car driver, and is slightly more practical and more comfortable. It is not short of spirit, however, with a top speed of 160mph.*

*The Griffith shares its chassis and thus its basic proportions with the Chimaera, although its styling is more dramatic. The superb leather interior adds a new dimension to the Griffith, and its shape reflects the themes of car's exterior design.*

*With its aggressive poise, the Griff has become the ultimate gentleman's sports car. Provided, of course, that you are a gentleman with an attitude. The sheer visceral thrill of the kick in the back and the howling exhausts when you put your foot down . . .* in veritas testiculae canis.

Cars shown here kindly loaned for photography by MOLE VALLEY TVR, CHESSINGTON, SURREY

one hurtled past. If this is where the local bikies come to play, I thought to myself, it must be a fun road.

Sure enough, it was. It wound and twisted and rose and fell, and then opened up for a stretch, then curled into hairpins again. It was great fun, and by the time we got to the other end of it I knew the Chimaera a bit better, and was quite happy to turn the wick down a bit and stop for a couple of photo sessions.

"I wonder where the hell we are?" said Ben as we ambled away from the Trough of Bowland and towards what seemed to be the Forest of Bowland. "Wherever it is, I think I want to live here."

A little green light began to flash on the dashboard, suggesting that it would be a smart move to put some more petrol in soonish. There were also audible empty warnings coming from my own internals, so I was delighted to spot a very attractive old Gothic pub nestling by the side of the road. The engine rumbled into silence, my stomach rumbled in sympathy and

***Above: Road testing the Chimaera on a challenging, entertaining road, listening to the overrun burbles and howling chords from the tailpipes. A tough job, but I suppose someone had to do it. Below: The stereo is probably quite good, but the exhausts make such a fabulous noise I didn't bother turning it on.***

***This is the view of the Chimaera that most people will see. The real reason for the half folded hood design is to shelter Chimaera drivers from all the envious V-signs from people who have just been overtaken because they aren't driving one.***

we wandered into the Inn at what turned out to be Whitewell. The entire building was cluttered with a welter of fascinating old stuff, as opposed to self-conscious 'antiques', which had nevertheless been assembled with considerable style and with a streak of surreal humour. The walls were covered in what looked like genuine sporting prints, and the back half of a stuffed fox stuck out of a hole in the wall.

Stone flags were eroded into soft curves by the shuffling of generations, and the entire place had a air of having been worn comfortably into shape.

"Peat fire in room £3 extra. Dogs with good manners and kind natures are very welcome. Approximately 8 miles of river is available to residents ... yerss, I think very definitely I'd like to live around here," muttered Samuelson, inspecting the tariff.

I could see his point. I was sitting in front of a nice big fire blazing away in a fireplace big enough to park a jeep in, nursing my allotted half pint of rather well-kept Marston. Only a half, of course; there are very things more redundant than a motoring writer with no driving licence. The menu looked imaginative and not too frighteningly expensive, and the ambience was generally pretty damn amiable.

When we asked where the nearest petrol was, they very generously said if you're really stuck we could get them to open the petrol station here. However, as it was only a few miles to the next nearest one, we decided not to bother them. There is still the odd pocket of civilisation left in this country, I thought to myself. I shall come back here for a weekend when resources permit. If I got to spend an entire weekend here with peat fire in room, £3 extra, and a nubile companion of the female persuasion, exploring the hills and working our way through the wine list and menu, you would not hear a barrage of complaints.

Be that as it may, it was time to call it a day and head back to Blackpool. Back into the cockpit, shut the door with a solid thunk, churn churn blast and we're off again, this time in the dusk. Blue sky reflecting purple highlights from the polished red bonnet and wings. Nice. Fat little steering wheel, designed to be gripped at the quarter to three position. Take it easy, particularly as the you-are-running-out-of-petrol light is flickering rather more insistently.

Bimbling along in top with the engine barely turning over reveals another aspect of the Chimaera; if you wanted to use one as a comfy long-distance transport, and just have the odd blast in it for fun, it would be a good car to use for that sort of travel. Very long-legged and relaxed. You could drive it for several hundred miles without getting tired, and that's unusual in a car with suspension that's stiff enough to give you this sort of handling.

There is an ideal balance between compliance for ride comfort, and stiffness for handling, and I think this TVR has probably got it about right. What made me think about the suspension was stopping for petrol – when the car came to a stop, there was no dip and rise of the body, the way there usually is when a car stops. The Chimaera simply stopped dead, with no movement of the bonnet at all. Likewise the rear; the only way you can get the back to dip significantly is by treating the throttle with considerable disrespect. A few gallons of super unleaded and we're reluctantly heading for Blackpool, cocooned in the snug beige leather, with the six instruments glowing and the exhaust crooning quietly to itself. Or at least as quietly as a TVR exhaust ever croons, which is not hugely quiet.

Did I have any complaints? Well, the indicator indicator is at the wrong end of the dash and isn't very bright, which isn't very bright, if you see what I mean and see what I mean. And the big central chassis means there's no extra room to rest your clutch foot. Otherwise, I thought, the Chimaera overall was superb, one of the best cars I've ever driven. *In veritas testiculae canis,* you might say. My only serious complaint was that they wanted it back.

*Following that, then, what's the direction for TVR now?*

Ah. Well, we're doing our own engine at the moment, and we're going to basically carry on in the same vein. That's quite a big investment, quite a big thing, and we'll carry on developing the cars in much the same format, and stabilise the market and carry on being reasonably successful.

*I suppose the new engine will take up a lot of time?*

Oh, I don't know. It has taken a lot longer than we originally thought, but that's only six months longer. It's now running, and it seems to be running to spec, so we're quite pleased at the moment. The only problem we've had with it is the last thing you would have expected, and that's been machining subcontractors. It's been making the bits fit together that's been causing the delays.

*The machining's all subcontracted out?*

Well, we don't yet have the full machining facility to make engines.

*From my own experience in the kit industry, it seems that British engineering companies tend to fall off sharply in quality after the first few pieces.*

No, I don't think that's the case with us; we're simply talking about putting holes in the right place. Once you've got the thing organised so that it can go on the latest type of machine tools, then the problem should disappear. No, all I'm saying is that machining's the last thing we expected problems with. Nobody would have expected us to make an engine from scratch that bears no relationship to any previous engine. All the areas that we did expect to provide difficulties have been relatively problem free.

*The AJP certainly looks beautiful, very neat, very elegant.*

Well, that's what we're trying to do.

*So, TVR cars will basically carry on becoming more refined versions of themselves.*

Well, they won't necessarily become more refined as such, but it's definitely our policy to take advantage of our strong points, and with our low tooling costs, we can produce new models at a fraction of the cost of everybody else, and that's where our strength is, so we'll carry on producing new models much as we do now. It's been suggested that we're going to do something like an MG, but that's not our intention. We make new cars to sell, rather than be led by any sort of marketing dream.

*You'll carry on with cars that are roughly the same size and shape, then?*

Roughly the same size and shape, yes. We have some grandiose ideas of making GT cars and having a go at Le Mans, that sort of thing, that's what we're considering at the moment.

*There's the new 2 plus 2 version of the Chimaera, isn't there?*

Yes, that's been market led by the lady who sells the cars here, and by our dealers, who say they could sell a lot of cars if there were room for kids in the back. I personally am not convinced of that at all – but it hasn't cost us an awful lot of money to do, so we've done it.

*Is it just moulding changes?*

No, the chassis's not exactly the same, because it's eight inches longer for a start, and it's had to be stiffened up because that cost 10% of its torsional stiffness, so we had to do quite a lot of alteration to get that back. It's not really the same chassis.

*That's a departure, then; earlier 2 + 2 TVR's used to just have dips in the floor moulding for theoretical feet ... what's the £60,000 V12 TVR I was reading about?*

It's not appeared yet. Whether it will or not, I don't know.

*What sort of a thing would it be?*

It would be the same sort of thing, but very very fast. Lots of horsepower, frightening, and a road racer type of car.

*A two seater in the Griffith style ... what sort of speed and power would it have?*

Speed I don't know. Power is fairly predictable, it would be around 500 horsepower. We never get to know how fast they are until we build one and get it road tested. This would be pretty nippy, though.

*Of course, the hands on method, where you build a car and physically see what it does, is a fraction of the cost of the sophisticated computer prediction approach, isn't it?*

Yes. Also we can change a lot faster than bigger manufacturers, because we don't have to budget five years ahead. At the moment, everybody and his dog is making four wheel vehicles for the niche market. It doesn't take a particularly clever person to see that falling around their ankles in a very short space of time.

*Is the boom in big jeepy things not a response to the flimsiness of current production cars?*

No, I don't think so. I think it's because of the relatively cheap pose value. It's fashion. Also, if you talk to the dealers, the boom in four wheel drive is very much fuelled by the same thing that fuels our car market – the very high secondhand prices. The secondhand prices of TVRs are very high indeed, so you're not taking a risk, and that was the case with four wheel drive vehicles. They held their value very well, but there are signs that that is not going to continue. As more and more come on to the market, market pressures take place, so that feeling of financial comfort may not last too long. The resale value is a major selling point with a TVR.

*Of course they don't really deteriorate, do they?*

We've sold a load of the new Griffith 500, and the majority of people who bought the 11-month production run of the previous Griffith have sold them for more money than they paid for them. Which is amazing at this point in a recession.

*I can't think of anyone else who's doing that at the moment apart from Morgan.*

I don't think even Morgan are doing that now. I don't think they're fetching premium prices. TVR is about the only one that is. Okay, that is a very good reason for buying another one, but you never know when that might change ...

*It's a considerable compliment, isn't it?*

I don't know if it is a compliment, it's to do with the demand for the car being larger than the supply. If we made ten thousand, I'm damn sure it wouldn't be the same.

*People do want them, though, don't they?*

They certainly want Griffiths, yes, and they've wanted Chimaeras very badly this year. We've had a tremendous year selling them. We had a good year last year with the Griffith but the Chimaera, without the hype, has probably outsold the Griffith this year. For the Griffith, we had this two year wait, and lots of presold orders from the show, with all the publicity. The Chimaera didn't have any of that. It just went into the showrooms, and the sales were terrific.

*The Chimaera does have a nice blend of traditional and new in it. But the sales of the traditional S have been dribbling off a bit, haven't they?*

Yes, they have now. Which shows a definite difference between our customers and say Morgan. Our customers aren't buying TVRs because they are traditional British sports cars – because the most traditional one we make, they aren't buying.

*There are elements of the traditional format which are still important to them, though.*

Obviously the format is very traditional, but people are – well, I think it's creating a new market. We wouldn't say we were selling to the traditionalists; that isn't the case as all. We obviously sell a lot of cars to TVR people, we have very high customer retention. Of the Griffith 500, maybe 70% of them have been sold to TVR owners. So that's a very nice steady market to have. But the new people ... let's put it this way; there is the odd Morgan traded in, but it's far more likely to be a Mercedes or a Jaguar. Which is very strange if you think about it.

*Yes, they are very different, aren't they?*

Very different. But I think that some of that goes back to people buying new cars in new ways in times of recession. They have the money to buy, but they're not prepared to see the value fall away very quickly. I still maintain that a Mercedes would be bought – apart from being a good car or whatever – because of the resale value.

*Of course, they were right up at the top for depreciation, weren't they. And now they're not.*

That's a very good indication of what people's buying habits really are, because a typical TVR customer can see what's what.

*So you can tell what makes are starting to depreciate badly by what your dealers take in part exchange?*

Oh yeah, all the time, that's always been the case. Putting it very crudely, if you start an export drive, as we did recently in France, all the first twenty customers have got Lotuses which they can't sell. But it happens with all cars, as I was saying about the four wheel drive – that's the danger to that market. Land Rover are very successful at the moment because secondhand Discoveries are worth a lot of money. People see that, and there are a lot of feelings about value for money involved. Much more than you would think. That's why Porsche made such an appalling marketing decision a few years ago when they discounted heavily on new cars.

*Marcos did the same thing, when they introduced the new Cortina based kit car. When you could get a genuine Marcos for a few grand and a dead Ford, that really hammered the value of second hand V8-and-leather-trim Marcoses.*

***This is a much better portrait of Peter. He doesn't usually say much, but it's always worth listening to.***

MG and people like Jensen, all the small manufacturers, have had similar problems too. What the hell is the point of paying £100,000 for a new Jensen when you can get a beautifully restored, perfect example for £20,000? It makes very little sense to pay £100,000 unless you've got more money than sense – and in a recession, people with more money than sense suddenly develop sense.

*Of course in a TVR you're offering an extremely unusual level of value, aren't you?*

Well, that's part of it, of course, we don't market the cars on competitors' value, we sell the cars on a cost-plus basis. We do not take any notice whatever of what anybody else is selling their cars for.

*And so people get a lot more car per quid from you.*

Well, we don't have Porsche's expensive marketing machine to support. If you pay £80,000 for a Porsche, it's probably cost not far off that to produce ... so it's the right price, if you like.

*The thing is, a company the size of Porsche with all their marketing, advertising dealer incentives, pension plans, finance, pot plants and so on – there's not much money left to spend on making cars, whereas pretty well all you do is make cars, isn't it?*

Yes, that's right, no waste motion.

*What is your most regretted might-have-been out of the TVRs that never came off? Any particular favourite that never got beyond prototyping?*

No, I'm not like that at all. I'm not a car nut. (Big grin) I can't think of a car that I regret not making, because if it didn't take off there was a reason for it. We've had a few goes at making things that might have been shown at the motor show, but none of them got very far unless they looked pretty promising.

*So the market knocks them on the head pretty quickly?*

Well yes, but there are about two or three people in the world who say what a TVR should be. We don't market test it at all, not even within the company. There's no outside marketing influence whatsoever. It's not done like that at all.

*I suppose new models are relatively minor swings off the main target, really.*

Yes. they become a styling and packaging exercise off an existing formula. And all the time, the power train and handling is developed independently. You asked what was my favourite car; probably from the point of view of engineering luck and skill, the best car by far we've ever produced is the Tuscan, because that was radically different from anything else we'd ever made. It had a very, very short gestation period: it was racing about four months after the idea was conceived. And the car was so right it wasn't true; if you built a car right now to the original spec, with the original dampers and springs and so on, it would still be competitive now, even after five years of development. So it was an amazing out-of-the-box design.

*And it has remained unchanged?*

Virtually no changes at all. People have spent loads of money trying to make them go quicker, but they've all failed.

*Mind you, they're already too quick for their handling, aren't they?*

No, I'm not sure that the case, no. If you made them more powerful, they'd go a bit quicker. I think the biggest difference is that people have learnt to drive them over the five years.

*Watching them try during the first year was hilarious, certainly.*

Yes, but if you look at it, some of the times set up on some of the circuits even then were quick. This last year's been the biggest difference, because Dunlop have changed the tyre compound. Not the size or whatever, but they had to change the way the tyres were made, for factory emissions or safety reasons or something. They didn't think it would happen this way, but the tyres are actually quicker. This is the first season that the lap records in the Tuscan series have been broken at virtually every meeting. Some of the lap records were standing from the first season. So from that point of view, it's a remarkable car. Plus the fact that obviously because of that, it spawned the Griffith and Chimaera chassis, which is very similar to the Tuscan. So that was probably the most right car we've ever done. In fact, it's probably the most right car for its purpose that anybody's ever done.

*Four months from start to finish.*

And that included building twenty, twenty-five cars.

*I always thought it was a shame that the Tuscan wasn't made as a road car; I think it's gorgeous.*

Yes, but it was designed not to be a road car, purely a racer.

*Certainly, I could see the point that by the time you'd turned it into a road car, you'd have put so much effort into it that you might just as well have started off with a clean sheet. I'd still love one, though. Just out of interest, what do you like in the way of cars that aren't TVRs?*

This is going to sound terrible, really. I quite like Range Rovers, because of the dog, and ... that's about it.

*Just the TVRs, then?*

Well, they're so similar to what I would have wanted if I'd been buying a car.

I probably don't drive competitors' cars enough, but the odd times I do ... I don't really have an opinion on them. One car I drove about a year ago, which was dismally unsuccessful, and when you drive it you can see why, which still had some endearing characteristics was a Maserati. It felt as though it was falling apart, and had some very peculiar characteristics, but I thought I might be one of the thirty odd eccentrics who might be interested in buying one.

*What was the sort of thing that formulated your taste in cars?*

The first sports car I had was a TR2. I had several, and I still think they're an exceptionally good car. That shows my age, I suppose.

*I had a favourite TR2 as well, but it fell to bits around me.*

Yes, that was one of the problems with them, but basically it was a good car. I never really went for the MGs, because the TR2 and TR3 were better cars.

*Well, of course it was designed as a car, wasn't*

*it? Whereas the MG was from the Austin A60 parts bins. Comfy, but a tourer rather than a sports car.*

Then from a styling point of view, I don't think Jaguar have done anything much better since the XK150. I used to like – although I'm not sure I still do – Astons a lot. Certainly the appearance of them I thought was fantastic, particularly the V8. When the V8 came out, I had one of those, and if you could get over the seven miles to the gallon, and the fact that the electrics were always failing, it was a nice car. I suppose going back a bit, the XK150 was certainly in its day a very fast and competitive car.

Mind you, I don't want to blow our own trumpet, but on the road – I'm not talking about going down the autostrada at 230 mph, but on the road across country, I think the fastest car you can currently buy is a TVR. I wouldn't want anything else. If something else came along that handled better and was significantly quicker, I might want one of those. I'm not a pure speed nut at all, though, really. Since I've been involved with styling the cars, I look at them and think I can't see anything else that I totally admire from a styling point of view. I thought, for example, and I can't have been alone because it's been very successful, that the Merc convertible was a nice looking car. I would never want one myself, because I can't stand the thought of fifty electric motors whirring away just to put the roof up. All that weight to haul around.

Also, I was following one the other day, and I noticed that the boot shut lines weren't particularly any better than a TVR, and the back of the hood design looks like some kid's drawn it. It wasn't until I really looked at it that I realised how amateurish it looked, and obviously nobody else sees it either. But nowadays I see things like that from a different viewpoint. From a distance it's a nice looking car, but when you actually look at it, it's not so wonderful. So I have this jaundiced point of view. I'm not saying that TVRs are perfect; when you've done them you always wish you'd done something else to them, but all I'm saying is that I can't think of anything which is absolutely stupendously styled or made or whatever. There's nothing that's outstandingly good from a handling or performing point of view. So overall, there's nothing modern that I really admire greatly.

Mind you, if someone wanted to put a nice 1935 Le Mans short wheelbase Aston in my garage, I would be extremely grateful and delighted. I'm tending as I get older to go that way. I can see what the design of that's all about, and I think it looks absolutely wonderful. A Speed 20 Alvis would be nice, too.

*Must admit, I'm the same. There's nothing among the moderns that I really want at all. Well, I would like a TVR, but not much else.*

Well yes, there's nothing that I can think of that I particularly desire.

*A lot of people I know in the kits and specials business seem to be doing better work in sheds than the*

**Wheeler racing a Tuscan at Brands, under considerable pressure from the white car behind him.**

*majors manage with budgets of hundreds of millions. Failing to make the current shopper significantly better than the last one.*

Certainly some of the current rear light treatments are kid's stuff. Horrible. I told the marketing director of one the majors the same thing. I think he secretly agreed with me, but because he was the marketing director he couldn't actually say so. He didn't argue very hard, let's put it that way. Mind you, I must admit that there's one of the new cars that's quite nicely done, which is one particular model of the new Corsa.

*The one with the blobby rear lights?*

Well, that one looks appalling, but there's another one which has those rear lights cut in half, it's a hatch or there's a gate on the back, and that looks very sweet. But how the same guy came up with the blobby thing, I don't know. It'll date very quickly. Okay for a gimmick, for a very short space of time. The half blob with the shutline through it looks very sweet, though. You can appreciate that someone did a good job on that. But when you look at the new cars around, there are very few like that. With all the technology they've got available, only a very few look right. But that's more and more evident on the mass produced cars, there are very few that have changed a company's fortune; the last one I can think of was the Peugeot 205. A very sweet looking small car. And that basically changed the whole outlook of Peugeot. The thing that amazes me is that everyone's still striving to do the same thing, and they will never succeed again. That will be the last time that one single car design, shape or whatever, will affect a major in such a way.

*Well, they're all pretty well indistinguishable now, aren't they?*

Yes. And what I'm saying is you get good and bad versions of the same shape. The back of an Escort looks terrible, but the back of that particular model of Corsa looks very nicely done. The guy or the computer programme that did that, got it right. Strange that the full blob version already looks dated to me. That's the problem with the Japanese cars. They've gone over the top into jellymoulds now, and that fashion will change.

*They all follow like sheep now, don't they? The computers rule ...*

They're all going that way. The Honda Civic, the one they race, is that the Civic?

*Um. I'm not sure which one that is.*

*At which point Ned stuck his nose in my ear, the telephone rang, and someone put their head round the door, so I took my cue and left Peter to get on with running the company.*

Chapter 12

# The Enthusiasts

The TVR owners' club was started in 1962, and was centred around a few friends in London. Since then it has grown to a considerable size, with 2300 members in the UK and a total of 3400 worldwide. "Worldwide" is literal, with members in New Zealand and Australia, all over Europe, and including the USA, Russia and Cuba. This would have been viewed with some displeasure and alarm by both the CIA and the Kremlin in 1962, and doubtless the King's Head, the Bull and the Swan would have finished up bristling with hidden microphones to catch the conversation at the monthly natter-and-noggin sessions. Even then, the TVR obsession would have taken over: even if the subject of a conversation was supposed to be poisoned umbrellas, torsion bars and gelcoat star crazing would have taken over before long.

The TVR club is now a limited company with three directors, and is modelling itself on the Lilley and Wheeler periods of TVR in its long term stability. If the club had followed the earlier pattern of TVR, of course, it would have collected 14 directors and gone bust. However, the current secretary has been a member and a committee member for ten years: his name is Roger Cook and he is the primary contact at the club. The other two directors are Mervyn Larner, the chairman, and Richard Adams, the treasurer. Roger is at pains to point out that although he and his colleagues are the figureheads, it's the unsung army of helpers who keep things going, not least of whom are a set of three very understanding wives. The club is genuinely open to any one who has a car with a TVR badge on it, at least as long as the badge was put there by TVR. The main financial advantage of joining the club is sensible insurance, arranged through companies who know what a TVR is. This way you get rates based on the genuine risk of covering one, rather than the insurers hearing the words GRP and V8 and sending Securicor round for the premium.

The 33 local regions organise monthly meetings and events for their own people, as well as getting together with other areas for bigger events. There are European events too, such as the three day annual meet at Zolder in Holland, and a German meeting at the Nurburgring. The club actually does very well for track days, with seven booked this year. The social side of things is good fun, but also brings very practical benefits – when you have a problem, someone in the club has invariably been there before. An example might be the rear windscreens on Vixens: even if the advice is, "Yes, it's a complete bastard and a living nightmare and it'll take all day," the next line usually goes, "If you want to have a crack at it Saturday we'll pop over and give you a hand." This is the stuff you want to hear when you're stuck.

The club also offer help with locating difficult and obsolete parts, and with obscure bits of information such as what colour your car was meant to be painted originally. Parts prices also come down a bit where the club is involved, and they understand the approaches and procedures of getting old registrations brought back to life at Swansea: the Guardians of the Bumf

***The TVR club race day at Brands Hatch. Every possible type of TVR is represented, including both Sixties and Nineties Griffiths.***

***Above: The author, belting cheerfully round Brands in a 1600 Vixen. This is about the most fun you can possibly have with your clothes on. Below right: Lining up for the off in the pit lane: S Convertible, Tuscans/Vixens, Griffiths, a Tasmin and an M series or a Taimar. Bottom right: The "Tuscan-Cobra" – a Vixen with a 289CI Ford V8 crammed into it. Hence the monster scoop and all the air holes across the front.***

have to be handled in a particular way. The membership of the TVR club is changing with the advent of the Griffith and Chimaera. TVR are now at the top of the specialist manufacturers' tree, and the attention they've had from the press recently reflects the tiny number of interesting and properly made cars available these days. It also makes people buy a TVR in preference to the usual Porsches and so on, so the flavour of the club has naturally had to change a bit. Where it used to be a bit of a cult of mostly M Series owners, the numbers of Griffiths are now increasing. However, the club hasn't been spoiled by this: the more the merrier as far as they're concerned.

Roger Cook is the archetypal TVR freak. He has been driving them since 1961. His Grantura, 287 JRT, recently underwent a thirteen-year rebuild. Well, it doesn't do to rush these things, does it? If you see a picture of a Grantura in a book or a magazine, it will usually be Roger's one. With that comprehensively seen to, his next task was to rescue the one existing Zante prototype, and to put it on the road. There was a chassis, a body, a 2500cc Triumph engine and box, and not a great deal more. The engine mounts were bits of wood, and the whole car was perched on a pile of old discarded bits and pieces. So far, he's got the engine and box properly fitted, suspension wishbones have been located and put on, the brake system is in and the body has been prepared for paint, all but the roof, which needs a little more flattening out before it's ready. As we go to print, Roger is trying to figure out where the cables, steering column and so on would have been intended to pass through the bulkhead, as none of that sort of thing was ever fitted.

The press shots of the Zante were quite convincing, but it was basiclly nowhere near finished. One of the few real problems is the windscreen. Most of the car's glass has survived, but the windscreen didn't. A Vixen with no windscreen is a problem, because you have to locate a screen for an early Fifties Mk1 Ford Consul. Tricky, but possible. The Zante, unfortunately, had its own special screen made for it. This was within TVR's budget, but not within Roger's: one-off compound curved windscreens are not cheap, in the sense that Van Goghs are not cheap. The current plan is to have a sheet metal plate made to the correct size, and then to have a plastic screen made by being heated and draped over the plate. This is not strictly kosher, and switching on the wipers would finish off the screen in pretty short order. Also, the car should not pass an MOT with a plastic screen. However, it is completely legal to submit it for an MOT with no windscreen at all. Like the spare tyre, if it's not fitted it can't be faulty.

Annual factory visits are organised by the club,

and their relationship with TVR is good: depite being generally as busy as an ants' nest, the factory always make time to talk to the club. The detailed records of what cars were fitted with what widgets and so on is sent to the club every few months, so that when someone drags an old Griffith out of a barn in forty years' time and wants to know what colour it should be, he'll only have to give the club a call. The number for the club is 0242 222878, and Roger makes a point of trying to get back to any caller within 24 hours, although he may come to regret telling me that. That number is the club office, and a message machine is left on when nobody's there.

The TVR Owners' Club must be one of the few institutions in England to be pretty well classless. At the 1993 Brands Hatch test day, there were absolutely all sorts of people there, all mingling cheerfully. A frightfully pukka type from Epsom wandered away from his two-day old Griffith, and was within moments deep under the bonnet of a manky old Vixen which was the pride and joy of a Northumberland garage mechanic.

Normally, any attempt at a conversation between the two of them would have been a pretty stilted affair, but the common interest in the dirty bits that lie beneath the bonnet of a TVR jumped the culture gap, and they were soon rabbitting away like childhood chums.

The spread of TVRs at that meeting was as eclectic as the drivers; if you'd closed your eyes and walked across the paddock, you would have tripped over many Griffiths, one Chimaera, a 420SEAC, a bunch of Tasmins of various sorts, one or two rare original Griffiths and Tuscans, a good few Vixens containing a variety of engines, a number of S Convertibles and Taimars, and even the occasional Grantura from the distant past.

A spluttering blast of noise, unmistakably the product of a decent sized V8, swung a good number of heads. The source was an old Vixen or Tuscan body with the legend 'Tuscan-Cobra' on the doors. The front of the bonnet sported as many holes as a government assurance, which in the case of the Tuscan indicated that there was something tasty concealed therein. Not actually a Cobra engine, as such, but it was definitely a 289 Ford V8, of the type which had been used in early Cobras, so at least it was semi-legitimate. The exhaust headers were pretty tortuous home made bag-of-worms affairs, winding around all over the place in a fairly tight engine bay. Still, the V8 was in and it was working, although after every four-lap blast around the circuit, the radiator was going PLFFFF in a fairly big way. I think it was probably nerves.

My own chariot for a bit of a spin round Brands was one of the old 1600cc Ford-powered Vixens from 1971. This one is kept by a chap called Gary, and is purely for racing. Its cosmetics are no more than adequate, and it's already been written off several times. The little red beast is given no quarter, and the resulting drive was quite fun. We must have been one of the lowest powered TVRs on the track, but by leaving the engine to reach valve-bouncing revs before smacking it into the next gear, and by braking very, very late and using every inch of the track, we made respectable progress, pressuring the more subdued drivers out of the way.

***Paul Pannack's 2500 Vixen before its rebuild: a fat cloud of oily blue smoke suggests that the end is nigh for the engine.***

The first close one came when some prat in a silver Tuscan overtook on the wrong side, and the second came when Gary overcooked it by just that extra tiny amount whilst shrieking around Druids, the nasty little hairpin at the top of the circuit. Out came the tail, round whipped the steering wheel, back came the tail – too far – BIG sideways slide, lots of blue rubber smoke, a bit more whirling of the steering wheel, a rude remark or two and the rear end was sufficiently back in line for a quick welly down the hill to tangle with the rest of the field again.

Was this fun? Do bears do whoopsies in the woods? Gary gets a lot more fun out of his motoring than most people, without putting any serious money into it at all. The bodywork gets repaired every time the car is pranged, the chassis is showing few signs of resentment at this sort of treatment, and the engine has now hung on for far longer than anyone could have expected. Gary's attitude is that it should already have blown up, and it undoubtedly will one day, but until then it will give of its utmost and then some. After all, it's only an old Capri engine, so replacing it will cost about as much as a speedo for a Chimaera.

Another pal of mine has for years had an obsession with TVR, which culminated in his taking me along to have a look at a 1972 2500 Vixen for him when it came up for sale a few years back. Having taken it for a spin, I reported that the steering kicked like a howitzer, the power was adequate and the handling was unbelievable; I also told him to buy it. He scrabbled frantically for a sufficiency of dosh, pawned a few cameras, and managed to scrape up enough.

That yellow Vixen kept going for years just as it was bought, but gradually the engine began to deteriorate beyond hope. It had been no spring chicken in the first place, and it had done thousands and thousands of miles since it had been bought. The oil consumption overtook the petrol consumption, the clattering got louder than the stereo, and eventually, with a rattling cough and a rich cloud of white smoke, the car ground to a final halt.

Knackered? I should say so. If you pushed the pistons to one side of the bore, you could see right down to the sump. The only reason there was any compression at all was the layers of gunge that had replaced the ground away bores. The crankshaft looked as twisted as an embarrassed python, and the crankshaft end float was measurable in thousandths of a yard rather than of an inch.

However, the body was still in remarkably good nick, with only a small amount of star crazing, and the chassis seemed to be pretty sound, too. Even the interior was all basically intact, although tatty. It was time for Paul to let his obsession really have its head, and he started pulling the car to pieces for total restoration.

Unfortunately, at that point in the recession things began to get somewhat thin for advertising

***Top: The renovated chassis – not that it neeeded much attention – sits in the Surbiton garage which it shares with the washing machine. Below: The introduction of an overdrive box meant that the handbrake had to be relocated slightly.***

***The 2500cc Triumph six was rebuilt and injected, to bring it up to 150 BHP TR6 spec and a little more...***

photographers, and coincidentally for advertising copywriters too, which is one of the reasons why I'm writing books instead; but that's another story. From the point of view of the Vixen, the days of ringing up David Gerald and asking them to bung a set of new wotsits in the post were now over, and any rebuilding on the TVR was going to have to be done the hard way.

As it turned out, the cylinder block in the car had been from a Triumph saloon rather than a TR6, so as it wasn't either original or correct, it was simply binned and replaced by a similar one in better basic condition. The big end and main bearings were changed, although they'd been in pretty good shape anyway. The pistons and rings were a bit shot, but the bores themselves were very good.

Six new pistons, however, were at that point rather a daunting financial problem, as that was about six more than Paul could afford. A friend and neighbour, who works on helicopter engines for a living, wandered in and admired the shiny red pistonless engine gleaming on the bench, and examined the rather sad looking pistons.

"I wonder," he said, picking one up and examining it closely. "Let me borrow one of these for a bit."

Shortly afterwards, he reappeared with six extremely shiny and gorgeous pistons, which turned out to have come from a rebuilt helicopter engine and which fitted perfectly. Helicopter engines have to be rebuilt periodically, whether they need it or not, as an engine failure tends to be unwelcome. However, a piston removed from a helicopter engine at the end of its life is generally in better shape than a car piston at the beginning of its life, so that was one problem conveniently solved.

Would the same technology apply to valves and guides, we wondered? Sure enough, it did. Again, the tolerances and clearances of aircraft engineering made the automotive components look as though they'd been hand carved by a ten-year old, and pretty soon the head looked as delicious as the block.

The old Triumph six is a good engine, but it has one or two peculiarities in its design. Firstly, all the oil drains down to the sump overnight, so when you start it up cold, there's a ghastly clatter from the bone dry bottom end of the engine. A non-return valve and a remote oil filter sorts that one out, however.

The other oddity is that the oil feed to the rockers is poor, and they tend to wear quickly for that reason. There are two blanked off holes in the engine, however, to which you can connect a pipe. This provides an extra oilway to the head, and saves the rockers from premature wear. However, this must mean less pressure available at the bottom end; I for one would rather hear a rocker rattling than the big ends. Why did Triumph block it off in the first place? Who knows.

Paul decided to go for oomph over originality, and started rooting out bits of TR6 injection gear at various autojumbles and club meets. Before long, he had a big enough pile of the stuff to be able to assemble a complete set of pumps and injectors that worked. There was no way a helicopter could be expected to yield a camshaft, so there was much grubbing in the depths of the pockets. Did Paul really need all those lenses for the Canon? Perhaps not *all* of them ... the cam was duly purchased and fitted with a vernier gauge on the end, which allowed very accurate cam timing.

The original diff had been sloppier than an office party kiss, and a very complex deal was done involving the original four-speed gearbox (good) being swapped for an overdrive box (not too good) with another diff (better) and a few other injection odds and sods.

The overdrive unit on the box interfered with the handbrake mounting inside the transmission tunnel, but after some judicious hacking, it looked as though it would go in okay. An attempt to flush through the radiator revealed the reason for the weekly attempts to solder up the continuous series of leaks; the whole thing was utterly bunged up with twenty years of coagulated crud, which showed no more intention of leaving the scene than Cilla Black. As the brasswork was almost thin enough to read through anyway, the radiator was abandoned and a new one was rooted out.

The body, in the meantime, had been hauled off the chassis, which could now be inspected for rust and damage. There was very little; the main rear beam across the back of the car was a bit crumbly, and the two outer side rails under the sills looked a little rough, but after they had been replaced they turned out to have been okay anyway. The rest of the chassis was still in good shape.

The body was inspected for cracks and damage, and any suspect bits were ground out and re-gelled. Overall, though, the main structure needed very little real attention. Considering the rebuild took several years, it's difficult to say where all the time went, although a lot of it was down to wallet-related project paralysis.

When the tide turned and the time finally came to

**_Getting the body off was easy. Just collect four people, promise them each a can of Scrumpy, put one person at each corner and heave._**

put the whole thing back together, step one was dead easy. Drag the engine and box over to the middle of the garage, lift the chassis over it, bolt it in. Ten minutes. Easy peasy. The suspension and so on went on easily too; it's always a bit of a luxury when everything's nice and clean.

The rebuilt, shotblasted and hot zinc sprayed front brake calipers looked almost good enough to eat, but Paul had forgotten to mask completely over the piston area. Getting the zinc off the bore surround without scratching the bore was one of the more challenging little jobs that resulted from the Vixen rebuild.

Springs and shock absorbers – six of them – came into the category of Not Cheap, but fortunately Quadrant Dynamics weighed in with a reasonable price on a set of their spring and shock combos. They use aircraft fluid in their shocks, which apparently works very well, but is vicious stuff if it ever gets out of the shock absorbers.

The rear suspension uprights were cast from aluminium, and they don't have the best reputation for longevity or toughness. Ask Gerry Marshall about how they used to cope with racing, but be prepared for some rude words. In this Vixen, the uprights were still in reasonable shape, which was a relief in view of their price.

The wheels were skimmed and fitted with a set of BF Goodrich radials. No particular reason for choosing them, except that they came as a bit of a bargain in another of the series of complex barter deals that had enabled the whole project to creep forwards. With that done, the chassis was at last mobile.

The body went back on without any bother at all; it was just a matter of collecting four individuals who were in a helpful mood, and plopping the body in place on the chassis. With that done, the problem of the wiring could be attacked. Most of the original loom was still in place, but it had been conceived by an artist rather than by a scientist in the first place; most of the colours of the various wires bore no logical connection to anything at all, except that some of the colour combinations along some of the bits of loom offered tasteful and quite pretty visual effects. However, as far as providing any indication as to what was supposed to connect to what, forget about it. Fortunately, around that time I wrote a piece on Sebring Healey replicas, who were then importing their kits from the States. Accordingly, a bit of serious photography was exchanged for a nice new wiring loom which could be adapted to suit the TVR, and which had the wires numbered rather than coloured.

The loom was unnecessarily complex, and quite a lot of it was simply deleted. Paul, during one puzzled phone call, asked what the hell I thought they could have meant by Back Up lights. Fortunately, I speak American, and I was able to tell him that Back Up means reversing lights.

***Top: Off she goes to the spray shop. Although it took some time to get a good surface finish, the bodywork was basically in very good condition despite its age. Above: A nice shiny coat of Renault yellow two-pack, very close to the car's original colour as specified by TVR.***

A new dash blank was cut from plywood, and a modelling photo session was exchanged for enough black leather to cover it. The seats were dealt with in a similar manner, and fairly soon the components of the refurbished interior were all to hand.

A technical college at Leatherhead with a car spraying course was persuaded to use the TVR body for demonstration purposes, and it was trailed up there for the students to practice their craft on it. The finish was to be the same rich yellow that the car had been in for some years, and which actually suits it very well. The students made quite a nice job of the preparation, and the two-pack paint job looked pretty good when the car finally came back.

The bonnet and hinge, measured and fitted with tedious care and attention only a month previously, no longer fitted. This situation was not physically possible, but was nevertheless the case. Paul started measuring again, but I said bollocks, measuring it is obviously the wrong approach, and is destined not to work. If we are to be inconvenienced by the laws of physics failing to apply, I said, we will have to subvert

***Paul Pannack, perched on the wing of his freshly finished pride and joy: very nice it looks too.***

the law.

This made sense to Paul, so we cut the hinge off the bonnet, bolted it to the chassis, perched the bonnet where we wanted it to go, and then bonded the hinge back onto it. Measuring, I am convinced, would just have made matters worse.

With the resulting car looking increasingly TVR-shaped, the next big bundle of laughs was getting the rear screen in. This is huge, and so expensive that even the Aga Khan would blanch. Despite having carried the same piece of glass for twenty years or so, the body was no longer remotely interested in any further association with it. There was much bending, twisting, hacking, kicking, grinding and bad language, but finally the screen reluctantly agreed to go back into place.

Door hinges were another source of amusement, as the original Ford Anglia ones had rusted out and collapsed. Towards the end of the TVR's previous life, the hinges had got so saggy that getting in had meant lifting the door up by the window frame and sort of throwing it at the door aperture, then sticking your arm out of the window and slapping the door until it clicked into place. (The inner door handles had already fallen off many years previously).

The original sunroof had been a folding Webasto number, but you can't have one of those in London because the natives will slash it, so a tinted glass one had been fitted. This for some reason always leaked, and still does, in spite of judicious applications of silicone goop. In the end, it's easier to dubbin the seats and keep a baling bucket in the car than to argue with it any further.

TVR had spent much time raiding the Ford parts bins for odds and sods of trim in 1972, and Paul found himself doing exactly the same at auto jumbles in 1992. Mark II Cortina door handles and rear lights are fitted, the lights upside down, and the bonnet side vents had originally graced the rear roof pillars on the same Ford. This nicking-bits-from-Fords business is still going on, which is rather a nice thought. Take a look at the back lights on a Chimaera, and then keep an eye open in a supermarket car park.

With a new Ford Consul windscreen fitted, the last part needed was a combined number plate and reversing light, last seen on a Rover P4 or a Triumph Vitesse; after some considerable rooting around, a good one was found, and the Vixen was heading for roadworthiness.

Watching Paul's face when he finally got to start his pride and joy up was quite fun; I think if he'd been given the choice of either going for a drive or being licked all over by a parliamentary research assistant, he'd still have reached his hand out for the keys.

TVRs seem to have a very strong appeal for most people who get involved with them. Certainly it was fun to get back behind the wheel of the little yellow beastie and to take it for a good thrash. There's now more than 150 BPH available, and the power delivery is as smooth as the Triumph six has always been. The suspension is exactly as brutish as it always was, and the steering still kicks like cheap Tequila, but you can still chuck the car round a right angled corner in the wet at unbelievable speeds with not the slightest hint of protest, apart from the centrifugal force throwing every loose object in the car over to the other side.

The Mike the Pipe exhaust still pours out a nice throaty throb, and the lumpy bonnet still points towards the horizon. from this Vixen to the current Griffiths and Chimaeras, the character of TVR remains unchanged, and their basic purpose is still the same. They are for enthusiastic drivers to use for going very quickly across country, and they've never lost that.

This is what links most TVR enthusiasts, whether in the club or not. Most car clubs represent particular subtexts and aspirations. For example, the Ford Capri and the Bentley owners' clubs are likely to have rather different memberships, and there's a strong element of nostalgia in a lot of clubs, and considerable snobbery involved in the Jaguar clubs. However, perhaps because a 1993 TVR is still intended to do the same thing as a 1973 TVR, and because that's why people buy them, the brotherhood of TVR people encompasses an unusually wide spectrum of individuals; and it's all the better for that.

Chapter 13

# The Might Have Beens

Unfortunately for devotees of trivia and enthusiasts of the oddball, most of TVR's might-have-beens are thought up, prototyped, evaluated and destroyed before anyone outside the company gets to see them. The size and nature of the company allows them to come up with an idea, give it a go, and then knock it on the head very quickly indeed. Not much of this activity is wasted, however; a series of bad or average ideas is part of the process of coming up with good ideas. Also, no car design has ever been a complete waste of time. Although the Zante never went into production, you only have to look at the first of the Tasmins to see what a profound effect the Zante concept had on it. Also visible in the Zante is the influence of Trevor Fiore's Trident design, particularly around the rear of the roof.

There was one Zante completed; this is now

*The Zante, at the Motor Show and on the road. Pretty revolutionary for the time, and with a bit of refinement it could have been very sexy indeed. Although it never went into production, we can see its heritage in the later Tasmin wedge.*

TVR
TVR 100

*The Tasmin Turbo. The late William Towns once told me that straight lines on motor car designs need to be handled with considerable care. I think he was right. Fast, the Turbo was: subtle it wasn't.*

under restoration by a private enthusiast, and we can look forward to its reappearance at some stage.

Another 'nearly man' was the Tasmin Turbo. Two of these were built, featuring peculiar, angular additions to the bodywork, and a 2.8 litre Ford V6. The output of the turbocharged engine was rated at 228 bhp at 5600 rpm, and the torque figure was 249 ft/lbs at 3200. Other mods to the wheels, brakes and so on had been carried out, and two prototypes were constructed. However, Peter Wheeler had never been a big fan of blown small engines, and preferred to start off with a decent amount of cubes and cylinders in the first place, and to go on from there. The Tasmin Turbo project faltered, and fell by the wayside.

***The Saloon got the thumbs down at the Motor Show, and was quietly wheeled back to Blackpool and disposed of. Camera angles here were carefully chosen to disguise the fact that the car only had one door.***

The TVR Sports Saloon was an idea that got as far as one Motor Show and then quietly dropped from sight. The prototype was never actually completed; when it was time to roll it on to the truck for the show, the shell looked finished, but it was short one door. Fortunately, they could pretend that

the door was deliberately missing to allow the public to get a look at the interior.

The car was 8" longer than the convertibles of the time, and had quite a decent sized boot. The running gear was intended to come from the 420. There was more head and leg room than that offered by the current Porsche 944, and there was a novel approach to headlights; rather than having the lights pop up, the whole front of the car moved to reveal them.

However, the response of the press and the public to the Saloon was total indifference, and it was discreetly wheeled back to Blackpool and disposed of.

One of the few prototypes that still exists is the car known as the "White Elephant". This is currently at TVR's Birmingham dealership, and was a mixture of a styling exercise and a test bed for the Holden alloy V8 made by General Motors in Australia. The American Ford 302CI Mustang had been tried, but with an iron block and heads, it weighed too much.

The 5-litre Holden engine produced about 250 bhp in standard form, which was fairly respectable. Also, a rather good electronic management system meant it was remarkably clean in pollution terms.

However, it had unusually big 'shoulders' and was thus tricky to get into the TVR without modifying the upper rails of the chassis. In addition, there was a

***Above: The White Eelephant. This Holden-powered special was driven by Peter Wheeler for some time, and is now undergoing restoration. Elements of Tasmin and 420 are visible in the design, and the dropped bonnet idea has now resurfaced in the Griffith. Below: The Holden engine fitted to the White Elephant. This was a small-block injected Australian General Motors V8, and quite a good engine, but with the smaller all alloy Rover engine on sale just down the road, the Holden made no commercial sense.***

***Above:** The first of the modern TVR designs begins to gel in this design study for the Speed Eight. This was a big and stylish car, but it was premature. TVR buyers still wanted maniac two-seaters at that point.*
***Below:** The two-seater version of the Speed Eight: big, beefy and rather handsome. The basic proportions are quite close to the current crop of TVRs.*

similar lightweight V8 freely available from just down the road, so it made little sense to rely on a supply chain that went to the other end of the world.

Thus the White Elephant and its Holden were used for a while, and then left to gather dust as the company forged onwards. The body styling on the Elephant is pretty radical, and it seems to have been based on a Tasmin coupe body, although there are bits of later cars in there too. The flip up at the trailing edge of the bonnet is 420ish, and the dash definitely looks as though it's out of a 420.

The White Elephant doesn't look like any particular TVR, but it would certainly never be mistaken for anything else.

I came across another prototype, the Speed Eight, while grubbing around in a shed at the factory, looking at a wicked little Cosworth-engined racer. A large, black lump loomed as the door opened. I clambered over assorted engines and piles of wheels, and there was a big, beefy and decidedly handsome TVR, of a type I'd never seen or heard of.

It was much bigger and longer than the usual TVR size, and it had a couple of child-size seats in the rear. The body shape at the front had a smoothed-off SEAC sort of look, with pop-up lights, and the back showed evidence of the styling ideas that

# About the Author

Iain Ayre was born in Glasgow in 1954, and has a low boredom threshold and a surreal sense of humour. When his school saw a limited future for him as a schoolboy, he left with alacrity, to find a sympathetic coterie of stoned deadbeats at Harrow Tech. Reluctant to leave, he became President of the Students' Union. Finally leaving Harrow with one E grade A level, a moustache and a broken heart, he tried to be sensible until the threat of a semi in Pinner set off the alarm bells, and he evaded the issue by taking a teaching degree.

Discovering that children were ghastly, he abandoned teaching and took up photography, specialising in location test shots for model agencies, and occasionally getting paid for them. Photography developed into design and writing work, and the world of advertising had an opening for a semi-talented waster. When the current recession left advertising dead in the water, he jumped ship and started writing increasingly manic and disconnected articles in the specialist car press.

Nobody sued: this encouraged him to continue, and the results have been seen in *Car Builder, Classic Cars, Which Kit?, Fast Ford, Motor Caravan World* and *Alternative Car World*. Books on the Ferrari 512TR and the history of Maserati are currently under way, as is the manufacturing of replicas of the most gorgeous motor car ever made, the XK120 Jaguar. After that, a spell of sedation will probably be in order.

# TVR: 1947 - 1975

More highly entertaining TVR reading is available in the sister volume to this book. *TVR: Success Against The Odds* covers in depth the extraordinary and fascinating early history of the famous marque between 1947 and 1975. Author Peter Filby has done an exhaustive job of unscrambling a remarkably complex story of trials, tribulations and ultimate triumph, producing an absorbing book that no TVR enthusiast can afford to miss!

For further information on *TVR: Success Against The Odds*, contact the publishers, **Mitchell-Filby Ltd., 1 Howard Road, Reigate, Surrey RH2 7JE. Tel: 0737 247922.**